The Gnostics

Other books by Sean Martin:

History
Alchemy and Alchemists
The Cathars
The Gnostics
The Knights Templar
A Short History of Disease

Film
Andrei Tarkovsky
New Waves in Cinema

The Gnostics

The First Christian Heretics

SEAN MARTIN

POCKET ESSENTIALS

This edition published in 2010
by Pocket Essentials
an imprint of Oldcastle Books
PO Box 394, Harpenden, Herts, AL5 1XJ

www.pocketessentials.com
Reprinted 2013, 2015

A CIP catalogue record for this book is available from the British Library.

ISBN
978-1-84243-339-3 (print)
978-1-84243-694-3 (epub)
978-1-84243-693-6 (Kindle)
978-1-84243-695-0 (pdf)

4 6 8 10 9 7 5 3

Typeset by Avocet Typeset, Somerton, Somerset
Printed and bound by CPI Group (UK) Ltd, Croydon, CR0 4YY

'But you will, as it were bewildered with astonishment, constantly stop your ears that they should not be defiled by blasphemies, and you will turn to flight, for you will find nothing to reply; but the foolish people will agree with you, indeed will come to love you, for you teach what is customary with them, but they will curse me, for I proclaim something new and unheard of.'

Simon Magus to St Peter, the Clementine *Recognitions*

Contents

Prologue: Egypt, December 1945

Muhammad Ali al-Samman and his brother Khalifah were collecting fertiliser for their fields when they found the books.

They had led their camels out to the base of the cliffs at Jabal al-Tarif, near the town of Nag Hammadi in Upper Egypt, to dig for *sabakh*, a soft soil they used on their crops, when they discovered a large red earthenware jar. They were at first afraid to break the jar open, fearful that an evil spirit might be trapped inside, but Muhammad, realising that there might be gold in the jar, summoned the courage to break it with his mattock. A golden cloud of dust escaped into the air, which for a moment seemed to confirm their fear that Muhammad had freed a spirit, but then, as the cloud dissipated in the breeze, nothing. They looked among the broken shards but, to their disappointment, Muhammad and Khalifah could not see any gold. All there was inside the remains of the jar were 13 old books, bound in leather. Muhammad wrapped them in his tunic and they led their camels back home to the village of al-Qasr. Muhammad's mother, thinking the books worthless, and perhaps even a source of bad luck, burned some of them in the oven. Within weeks it became clear that the books the brothers had found at the cliff were not worthless, but of extraordinary value. By that time, however, both were being investigated for murder.

Six months earlier, their father, who was also called Muhammad Ali, had disturbed a thief during his shift as a nightwatchman guarding irrigation equipment out in the fields. During the struggle, Muhammad killed the man, but by mid-morning had himself been killed in revenge. Shortly after the books had been brought home, Muhammad received a tip-off that his father's murderer, a man named Ahmad, was selling molasses near their house. Muhammad alerted Khalifah and his other brothers, took their mattocks and, finding Ahmad asleep beside his jar of molasses, hacked him to pieces. In the final act of blood revenge, they cut out his heart and ate it.

Although Ahmad had been the son of the local sheriff, he had been so unpopular that no one came forward to testify against Muhammad and his brothers. They did, however, have to contend with the police, who started making nightly calls on the family home in al-Qasr to question them. Fearing that the books would be impounded, Muhammad asked the local priest, Basiliyus Abd al-Masih, to look after them. The books then came to the attention of Basiliyus's brother-in-law (Coptic priests being allowed to marry), Raghib, who taught English and History in al-Qasr once a week. Raghib persuaded Basiliyus to let him take one of the books to Cairo to get it valued, and Basiliyus consented. When Raghib arrived in Cairo, he took the book to George Sobhi, a Coptic doctor he knew whose passion was the Coptic language in which the book was written. Sobhi took one look at what was on his desk, and immediately called the Department of Antiquities.

Raghib was eventually paid £300 for the book, of which he had to donate £50 to the Coptic Museum in Cairo, who entered the book into their collection of antiquities on 4 October 1946. What they now had in their possession were ancient Gnostic texts, such as the Apocryphon of John, the Gospel of the Egyptians and the Dialogue of the Saviour, which were long believed to have been lost when the Church virtually erased the heretical Gnostics from the history books in the early centuries of the Common Era. The hunt was now on for the remaining 12 books, or codices as they came to be called, but by the time the Department of Antiquities started to make their enquiries in al-Qasr, the books had gone.

It transpired that Muhammad's neighbours – all of whom were illiterate – had acquired the remainder of the books for next to nothing. One, Nashid Bisadah, got a gold merchant to sell his book in Cairo and they divided the profit; another, a grain merchant, sold his in Cairo for so much money that he was able to set up a shop there. The remainder went to Bahij Ali, one of al-Qasr's more fearsome characters, who had one eye and something of a reputation for being an outlaw. Bahij, too, tried disposing of the books in Cairo, but nobody would touch them until he came upon a certain Phokion J. Tano, a bookdealer who promptly bought everything Bahij had. Although he didn't know it at the time, Phokion would not have the books for long. The Department of Antiquities soon called on him and impounded the collection to prevent any more of it leaving the country. When Nasser became President of Egypt in 1956, the collection was nationalised and handed over to the Coptic Museum.

Meanwhile, most of Codex I – including the Apocryphon of James, the Gospel of Truth, the Tripartite Tractate and the Treatise on the Resurrection – had been smuggled out of Egypt by Albert Eid, a Belgian antiquities dealer based in Cairo. He offered it for sale in New York and Ann Arbor in 1949, but there were no takers. The unsuccessful sales did, however, bring the codex to the attention of the noted historian of religion from the University of Utrecht, Professor Gilles Quispel, who urged the Jung Institute in Zurich to buy it. Negotiations took longer than expected, mainly due to Eid's untimely death, but on 10 May 1952, the Jung Institute bought the book from Eid's widow and took it back to Zurich, where it was given to the psychologist Carl Jung, who had a strong interest in Gnosticism, as a birthday present; from that time on, it became known as the Jung Codex.

Quispel, however, realised that there were pages missing from the codex, so he went to Cairo in the spring of 1955 to see if he could locate them. The Coptic Museum had the missing pages in its collection and allowed Quispel to borrow photographs of them. Returning to his hotel room, he began to read. The text began, 'These are the secret sayings which the living Jesus spoke and which Didymos Judas Thomas wrote down. And he said, "Whoever finds the interpretation of these sayings will not experience death."'[1] He soon realised that what he had in his hands was the complete text of the Gospel of Thomas, a partial Greek edition of which had been found during excavations in the Egyptian town of Oxyrhynchus in 1898, and which had been known since then as the Logia Iesu, or Sayings of Jesus. Unlike the four canonical gospels, Thomas is a compilation of Jesus's sayings, and Quispel could see some that were very close to the New Testament, such as saying 33, 'What you hear with your ear, preach in others' ears from your house-tops. For no one lights a lamp and puts it under a bushel nor does he put it in a hidden place, but he sets it on a lampstand so everyone who comes in and out may see its light,'[2] which has clear echoes in the Sermon on the Mount.[3]

However, as Quispel picked his way through the text, he could see emerging a Jesus who was at other times very different to the Jesus of the New Testament. The Prologue, for instance, claims that it records Jesus's *secret* sayings. Quispel wondered whether these were the sayings that the Gospel of Mark refers to when it describes Jesus's use of parables: 'He would not speak to them [crowds] without using parables, but when he was alone with his disciples, he would explain everything to them.'[4] The Prologue also announces that it was written down by Jesus's twin brother Thomas (Didymos being Greek for twin). Could Jesus really have had a twin brother? The canonical gospels mention that Jesus had siblings,[5] but only John, whose writer has long been thought to have drawn on different material than the writers of the other three canonical gospels, refers to 'Thomas (called the Twin)'.[6] Could the Gospels of John and Thomas have been privy to information that was denied to the other gospel writers? Elsewhere, the Gospel of Thomas portrays a Jesus more mystical even than John: 'Jesus said, "If the flesh came into being because of the spirit, it is a wonder. But if the spirit came into being because of the body, it is a wonder of wonders. Indeed, I am amazed at how this great wealth has made its home in this poverty.'[7] In Saying 70, the message is more radical still: 'Jesus said, "If you bring forth what is within you, what you have will save you. If you do not have that within you, what you do not have within you [will] kill you."'[8]

By the time Quispel had finished studying the text, it had become clear to him that what Muhammad Ali and his brother had found at Nag Hammadi was a wealth of early Christian material whose very survival and discovery meant that the history of the early Church – and possibly Christianity itself – would have to be rewritten.

Gnosticism and Christianity

The term 'Gnostic' has traditionally referred to the various groups which flourished in the early centuries of the Common Era and which stressed the importance of *gnosis* – direct inner knowledge of God – above dogma. The early Church Fathers condemned them as heretics and, until the discovery of the Nag Hammadi Codices, it was largely through their tirades against Gnosticism that the various Gnostic teachers and schools were known.

The word 'Gnostic' comes from the Greek word *gnosis*, 'to know'. The Greeks, however, differentiated between two types of knowing: one was an intellectual knowing, such as 'I know there is an Oracle at Delphi', where knowledge is garnered from sources outside oneself (for example, reading books or talking to other people and, in our era, watching television or using the Internet); the other type of knowing is of a direct, personal, intuitive kind, through which one could say 'I know what the Oracle at Delphi said to me', because you had actually gone to Delphi and had a direct encounter with the mysteries of the Oracle. It is this second type of knowing that is the hallmark of Gnosticism. The psychologist Carl Jung, who, as we shall see, was something of a Gnostic himself, put the Gnostic view very simply when interviewed for a BBC television programme in 1959, when he had had a lifetime's experience of studying Gnostic thought and texts. When asked whether he still believed in God, Jung replied, 'I could not say I believe. I know.'

Despite the writings of the early Church Fathers, most of whom were fanatics with an axe to grind, the term 'Gnostic' was not universally used by Gnostic teachers such as Valentinus and Marcion, who usually simply referred to themselves as Christians, nor by Church apologists such as Tertullian and Irenaeus, who often called them simply 'heretics'. The problem is further compounded by the fact that the Gnostics themselves were comprised of diverse groups which did not have a uniform set of beliefs; indeed, diversity is one of the hallmarks of Gnosticism. Furthermore, not all Gnostics were Christian – some were Jews, some Pagan.

Modern scholarship is divided over what is actually meant by the term 'Gnosticism'. In 1966, a colloquium of scholars met at Messina in Italy to establish exactly what is meant by Gnosticism and *gnosis*. They concluded that Gnosticism refers to the religious systems developed in the early centuries of the Common Era, while *gnosis* is the attaining of knowledge. One could therefore have *gnosis*, but not be a Gnostic. (For the present book, we will try to adhere to the Messina definitions.) The political theorist Eric Voegelin further muddied the waters when he attempted to define Gnosticism as being derived from a general feeling of alienation and disconnectedness with society. As a result, he detected Gnosticism in Marxism, Communism and Nazism, all of which, according to Voegelin, were movements which wanted to bring about apocalypse (he dubbed it 'immanentising the eschaton').

Gnostic tendencies have since been spotted in a wide variety of writers, thinkers, political and spiritual movements, and also across the spectrum of popular culture, from Hollywood movies to computer games and comics. This bewilderingly diverse group includes the likes of not only Jung, but also William Blake, Goethe, Herman Melville, Albert Camus, Hegel, Nietzsche, WB Yeats, Franz Kafka, Existentialists, all manner of Theosophists, Jack Kerouac, Philip K Dick, computer games such as the *Xenosaga* series, comics such as Neil Gaiman's *Sandman* and Alan Moore's

Promethea and movies such as *The Truman Show* and the *Matrix* trilogy.

In order to understand what links all these people, we need to take a long, convoluted and sometimes fragmentary journey that starts with early Gnostic seekers living at the height of the Roman Empire and ends – if this journey ever has an end – with people in a darkened movie theatre watching Keanu Reeves see the words 'Wake up, Neo' appear on his computer screen. For 'waking up' – just like Jung's 'knowing' – is precisely what Gnosticism is about and is precisely why it remains relevant to us today, perhaps more so than ever.

The First Christian Heretics?

Until the discovery of the Nag Hammadi Codices, most of the information we had on the Gnostics was derived from the writings of the early Church Fathers, who regarded the Gnostics as heretics. The earliest Christian apologist to deride the Gnostics was Justin Martyr (*c.* 100–c. 162), whose Second Apology condemns the figures of Simon Magus, Valentinus and Marcion as 'wicked and deceitful'.9 Irenaeus, the Bishop of Lyon (*c.* 130–202), writing in the late second century, saw Simon Magus as the original Gnostic, the 'Father of All Heresy', and therefore as the emerging Church's primary enemy.

Like most Gnostic figures, little is known about Simon other than through the writings of his opponents – men like Irenaeus and Justin. Simon first appears in Acts 8.9–24, where he is depicted as a Samaritan magician who is converted to Christianity by the apostle Philip. When the apostles Peter and John confer the Holy Spirit upon believers through the laying-on of hands, Simon asks if they can sell him their power. Needless to say, Peter and John refuse Simon's request, and Simon's sin in trying to buy divine power subsequently became known as Simony. Although Simon's appearance in the New Testament is brief, he also figures in the apocryphal Acts of Peter, where he is depicted as engaging in a series of magical battles with St Peter and for attempting to get Peter to not believe 'in the true God but in a fallacious one',[10] suggesting that Simon was trying to inform Peter that the true God and the creator God were not one and the same. (This is a central belief of Gnosticism, to which we shall return in due course.)

There were other aspects of Simon's life and teaching which were Gnostic, not least his claim to be God incarnate, which reflects the Gnostic belief that we all have a divine spark within us – we are literally part of the true God – and in his relationship with a woman named Helena, whom he had found in a brothel in Tyre. Simon had redeemed Helena and came to regard her as the human embodiment of Sophia, the divine wisdom. Needless to say, the early Church Fathers positively foamed at the mouth at the mere mention of Simon's name, especially as his teachings became more popular during the course of the second century. Indeed, Irenaeus felt that Simon's teachings had proliferated woefully and he mocked the Gnostics for the sheer number of tracts they wrote, claiming that they produced 'a new gospel every day'.[11]

For Irenaeus, the teachings of the Gnostics were an 'abyss of madness' and texts such as the Gospel of Truth were 'full of blasphemy'.[12] The Christian polemicist Hippolytus (d. 235) felt compelled to 'expose and refute the wicked blasphemy of the heretics'[13] in his epic *Refutation of All Heresies*. Of the various heretical groups Hippolytus condemns, over 30 of them were Gnostic. Tertullian (c. 155–230) lambasted the Gnostics for their denial of the physical reality of Christ's resurrection, declaring that anyone who did not believe that Jesus rose bodily from the grave was a heretic, and famously declared that the resurrection 'must be believed, because it is absurd!'[14]

To understand fully why figures such as Irenaeus took the positions they did, we need to set their remarks in the context of the time, which will show that there is a great deal more to the attacks on the Gnostics than is initially apparent, and which actually makes the emerging Church's position far less tenable.

The Origins of Christianity

Unlike today, Christianity in the early centuries of the Common Era was a mixed bag of beliefs and practices. Immediately during and after Jesus's ministry (which is traditionally held to have occurred between the late twenties and mid thirties CE), his followers were a minority persecuted by both the Romans and the Pharisees alike. There is continuing controversy as to who was Jesus's successor in the movement. Peter is traditionally seen as the Rock upon which the Church was built,[15] and from whom the Roman Catholic Church claims descent, holding Peter as the first Pope.

However, this is where problems set in. It has been argued[16] that Jesus's brother James, known as James the Greater, was the head of the first post-Crucifixion Christian community in Jerusalem and it is thought that James's followers clashed with Christianity's most fervent missionary, St Paul. This becomes all the more important when one recalls that Paul's ideas played a large part – indeed, one of the largest – in forming the theology on which the Christian faith is based. And yet he remains a controversial figure: he only quotes Jesus on one occasion,[17] and his letters – which form the largest part of the New Testament – are frequently addressed to other Christian communities clarifying points of doctrine or urging them to toe the line. Had early Christianity been a unified whole, there would have been no need for such letters. It would not be going too far to say that 'Paul, and not Jesus, was... the Founder of Christianity'[18] and therein lie the origins of Christian heresy: 'Paul is, in effect, the first "Christian" heretic, and his teachings – which became the foundation of later Christianity – are a flagrant deviation from the "original" or "pure" form.'[19] He is the 'first corrupter of the doctrines of Jesus'.[20] Jesus preached the Sermon on the Mount, Paul preached Christ Crucified; there is a big difference.

Perhaps the next most seminal figure after Paul is Irenaeus, who was the first to preach the 'Four-formed gospel' of Matthew, Mark, Luke and John, as they were the oldest gospels and therefore seen as the most 'accurate.'[21] Four was also a convenient number, as there were four winds and four directions on the compass. Unlike Paul, who initially persecuted Christians but was famously converted to the faith when he experienced a vision of Christ on the Road to Damascus, Irenaeus was born into a Christian family and remained a devout proselytiser all his life. He entered the Church in Lyon and was taught by St Polycarp, who had himself been a student of St John. Irenaeus, perhaps inevitably, became a fierce champion of the Fourth Gospel, and although he regarded Christian orthodoxy as being based on the four canonical gospels of Matthew, Mark, Luke and John, it was the latter that was 'the *first and foremost* pillar of "the church's gospel"... because John – and John alone – proclaims Christ's *divine* origin'.[22]

Irenaeus may have also been reacting against the Gnostic teacher Marcion, who argued that the Gospel of Luke was the only true gospel and even went as far as producing his own version of it. Another second-century Gnostic, Tatian, who had studied under Justin Martyr but then became a follower of Valentinus, rewrote all four canonical gospels into a single work, a text known as the Diatessaron. As we have seen, the Gnostics were mocked by the early Church Fathers for their ability to produce 'a new gospel every day', but this would appear to be a misunderstanding of the Gnostic position, which generally held that the writing of such texts was the proof that the true God was speaking through the believer and that what the true God had to say could never be confined to just four gospels, canonical or otherwise.

Generally speaking, each of the early Christian schools of thought would champion one gospel over all the others; even Irenaeus himself did so, as we have seen. Thus followers of Paul would hold that his writings were gospel, to pardon the pun, while the followers of Mary Magdalene would regard the Gospel of Mary as the main source of spiritual guidance. Still others would esteem the Gospel of Philip, the Gospel of Truth or the Gospel of Judas.

The Gnostic schools had other hallmarks in addition to their gospels. They were, in the main, anti-authoritarian and anti-hierarchical, with some, such as the Valentinians, taking it in turns to officiate during services.[23] If that wasn't bad enough in the eyes of the Church Fathers, they also regarded women as the equal of men and had female priests. Women were therefore drawn to Gnosticism as it offered them a genuine chance to participate. Others who did not enjoy the status of first-class citizen, such as the poor and outcast, were also welcomed. Gnosticism drew those who were disaffected and appealed especially to city dwellers who felt that conventional forms of religious expression had little or nothing to offer them.

The Origins of Gnosticism

The Gnostics themselves kept no official histories – it was simply not of interest to them to document how and why their philosophy began, the main focus of their teaching being *gnosis*. Scholars are therefore still debating the origins of Gnosticism. It is traditionally thought to be a form of Christianity that flourished in the first centuries CE, and that is certainly the impression one gets from reading the Church Fathers. In fact, it is a slightly misleading assumption, as Gnosticism probably had its roots in – or at least was influenced by – Jewish, Pagan and Iranian traditions that predate Christianity.

Judea in the two centuries before Christ was a hotbed of political and religious fervour, with Judaism itself evolving during this time. Once the Babylonish Captivity had ended and the exiled tribes had returned home in the late sixth century BC, friction was generated between them and the tribes who had stayed. The exiles felt that they were the true children of God, as they had remained true to the Torah and had suffered the punishment of exile to prove it, while the tribes who had remained in Judea were felt to be collaborators. Matters came to a head in 168 BC, in what was known as the Revolt of the Maccabees, which was sparked off by the Seleucid ruler of Israel, King Antiochus Epiphanes, when he embarked on an anti-Semitic purge. Rebellion quickly spread, Antiochus's forces were defeated, and the hard-line descendants of the former exiles gained control of the Temple in Jerusalem. To them, the likes of the liberal pro-Hellenic Hasmonean dynasty were as much the enemy as the Seleucids, and the general air of political turmoil led to a growth in fanatical groups of various persuasions.

These groups were frequently ascetic and apocalyptic, standing at the fringe of Jewish life. Perhaps the most well-known of them were the Essenes, a radical group based in the caves of Qumran overlooking the Dead Sea. It has been suggested by various writers that both John the Baptist and Jesus Himself were at one time members of the Dead Sea community – or at least were influenced by it – before beginning their respective ministries. While this is debatable, it is known that the Essenes sought to establish a new covenant with God, as they believed that Israel's sins had all but invalidated the old covenant (given by God to Abraham). According to Roman historians like Josephus and Philo, the Essenes were divided between those who had taken full vows – which involved living at Qumran and adhering to a strict life of celibacy, prayer and ritual – and those who were associate members who, while believers, lived in towns, plied ordinary trades and married.

In further foreshadowings of Gnosticism, the world view of the Qumran Sect was essentially dualist, in that they saw the world as the battleground between the forces of heaven and hell, and that man himself is the microcosm of this war: 'the spirits of truth and falsehood struggle within the human heart… According to his share in truth and right, thus a man hates lies; and according to his share in the lot of deceit, thus he hates the truth.'[24] They also insisted that what mattered was not one's ethnic origin — be it Jewish or Gentile — but one's morality: only the pure of heart would be saved.

Like the subsequent Gnostic schools that grew up in their wake, the apocalyptic sects taught an 'esoteric, revealed wisdom, and the resulting knowledge has an immediate relation to redemption. The knowledge of God's mysteries guarantees salvation; knowledge, or cognition, and redemption are closely connected.'[25]

Given that God's mysteries have to be worked for, the Jewish apocalyptic school was necessarily elitist; not everyone would be saved, but only those who were active on the spiritual path. The apocalyptics, like the Gnostics after them, regarded themselves as strangers in a strange land. They looked forward to the ending of historical time, at which point eternity and salvation would begin; the Gnostics, on the other hand, were in the main not so much concerned with the end of the world, as, for them, salvation occurred at the moment *gnosis* was achieved.

The Gnostics seem to have inherited a number of other beliefs from the Jewish schools. Both have a dualistic world view, as we have noted, which requires a belief in two gods rather than one. The god who created the world is not the same as the true God, who remains forever beyond the material plane. The creator God is often portrayed as at the very least incompetent, if not actually evil. His minions are known as archons, spirits who keep man in thrall to the material world and ignorant of his true nature.

Another strand of Jewish spirituality which may have contributed to Gnosticism is the so-called Wisdom tradition, which flourished between the fourth and first centuries BCE. The Old Testament book of Proverbs belongs to this tradition, as do the apocryphal Ecclesiasticus and the Wisdom of Solomon. In texts such as these, the figure of Wisdom is personified as being feminine, and as having a close relationship with God. 'She protects her own and helps them to the knowledge of God; she is like a redeemer who grants immortality.'[26] The Wisdom teachings also have an air of pessimism about them, in which God's actions are 'strange and inscrutable. He is removed into the distance and placed high above earthly concerns so that his acts in history and acts of creation become veiled.'[27] 'The Gnostic world view could take root and flower on this soil.'[28]

Two other religious traditions may have fed into Gnosticism: the Iranian/Zoroastrian and the Greek. Zoroastrian concepts such as a Day of Judgment, resurrection and dualism also recur in Gnostic thought. Zoroastrianism is usually held to be the first major world religion to espouse a dualistic view of the world. The prophet Zoroaster (also known as Zarathustra) founded what he called the Good Religion, or Zoroastrianism, some time in the second millennium BCE. The dates of his mission are unclear, and it has been placed in various epochs, from 1700–1400 BCE to 1400–1000 BCE or 1000–600 BCE. Current research tends to suggest the middle dates, making Zoroastrianism the world's oldest revealed religion, a religion that 'has probably had more influence on mankind, directly and indirectly, than any other single faith'.[29] Zoroaster was 'the first to teach the doctrines of an individual judgment, heaven and hell, the future resurrection of the body, the general Last Judgment, and life everlasting for the reunited soul and body'.[30] All of these ideas were to influence Gnosticism (to say nothing of Judaism, Christianity and Islam).

Zoroastrianism also has a unique solution to the problem of evil. In its traditional form, the Good Religion holds that there is one good god, Ahura Mazda (Wise Lord), under whom are the two equal twin forces of Spenta Mainyu (the beneficent or holy spirit) and Angra Mainyu (the hostile or destructive spirit). Although Ahura Mazda's creation is good, the source of all evil within it is caused by Angra Mainyu, who is destined to be overcome at the end of historical time, at which point eternity will begin. Classical Zoroastrianism, however, underwent changes as the fortunes of the Persian Empire rose and fell. Over time, Ahura Mazda became identified with Spenta Mainyu, reducing the original trinity to a binary pairing. The names of the Wise Lord and his adversary also underwent transformation, being contracted to Ohrmazd and Ahriman respectively. By the time of the Achaemenid Dynasty (550–330 BCE), Ahriman was no longer seen as being created by, and inferior to, Ohrmazd, but was now regarded as his equal.[31] Again, this concept of two gods would resurface in Gnosticism, where the true God remained outside of the world of matter, while the creator God was seen as arrogant and inefficient. This god came to be identified with the God of the Old Testament, suggesting that some elements within Gnosticism may have been rebelling against their Jewish heritage.

The lesser, creator God became known as the Demiurge, which suggests the influence of Greek thought on Gnosticism, 'Demiurge' being derived from the Greek *demiurgos*, meaning half-maker, while the word '*gnosis*' itself is, as we have seen, also Greek. Greek culture dominated the Western world until the advent of the Roman Empire, and this is particularly true of its philosophy. Indeed, the 'vocabulary of most of the Gnostic systems... derived from the conceptual language of Greek philosophy'.[32] Much of what concerned the Greeks, therefore, also concerned the Gnostics: the nature of God, the soul and the world; the Demiurge and the 'unknown God'; the origin of evil; the descent of the soul into matter and its eventual return; the dualistic split between mind and matter; fate and freedom. Whereas the Greeks addressed these issues rationally, the Gnostics tended to mythologise and elaborate, as we shall see when we look at the Gnostic creation myths in the next chapter. However, without the climate of enquiry established by Greek thought, Gnosticism may have either been unable to flourish, or would have developed in an entirely different way.

Another theory as to the origins of Gnosticism posits that it was, in fact, an entirely new religion that deliberately combined elements of Jewish, Iranian and Greek tradition into a new, syncretistic whole. For instance, features of Greek mystery cults such as Orphism could have played a part in forging Gnosticism. The Orphic cult – said to have been derived from the mythic figure of Orpheus – has a number of interesting parallels with Gnosticism: according to Orphic belief, when Dionysus was torn apart by the Titans, shards of his divine nature fell into all human beings, who had yet to be created. When people *did* finally appear, they had Dionysus's nature within them, often without their realising it. Only those who joined the Orphic cult could be freed from the prison of their earthly existence, which would entail observing cultic practices such as vegetarianism. It was an esoteric approach to salvation; those who did not join the cult would not be saved. Such elitism, which may at first appear politically incorrect to today's spiritual seekers, would also be a feature of Gnosticism and, as we shall see, some of their persecutors.

There are, of course, counter-arguments to suggest that Gnosticism could not have possibly been a syncretistic religion cobbled together from east and west like some old quilt. Stuart Holroyd sums this up eloquently:

> If it had been merely a synthesis of diverse traditions and ideas with some intellectually exciting or interesting innovations its appeal would have been superficial and ephemeral. It would have lacked the emotional and spiritual element without which [it would have been] lifeless and barren.[33]

Regardless of how Gnosticism evolved – the Gnostics themselves were not concerned with their own origins – evolve it did, and by the time of the second century CE, it was more theologically and philosophically advanced than the fledging Church, which regarded the Gnostics as the biggest threat it had yet faced. Gnostic beliefs are considerably better known than the mysteries surrounding their origins and it is to these that we will now cast our gaze.

Beliefs and Myths

The second century CE was the heyday of Gnosticism. It was the era of great teachers such as Marcion and Valentinus, when the dividing lines between heresy and orthodoxy had not yet been drawn, so much so that Valentinus, who is now regarded as one of the greatest of all Gnostic teachers, almost became pope at one point (probably in the 140s). Cities like Alexandria and Rome were alive with spiritual debate and enquiry: tracts would be written and circulated and groups would form around one teacher or gospel. This would inevitably lead to detractors circulating counter-claims and forming other groups; it was nothing if not colourful. In keeping with this tradition, we shall examine some of the key beliefs of Gnosticism and compare them with what was to become orthodox Christianity.

Gnosis

Many Gnostic groups had a habit of disagreeing with one another over doctrine – the whole concept of a rigid hierarchy of belief being something of an anathema to them – but they did all agree on one fundamental point, that of the importance of *gnosis*. As we have already noted, the kind of knowledge *gnosis* refers to is a direct, experiential knowing – a knowing in the heart as opposed to the head. It is non-intellectual and non-rational; it can only be experienced, not explained. Rather than making the world a more complicated place – as intellectual and theological arguments tend all too often to do – *gnosis* has the effect of liberating the soul. As the Gospel of Truth puts it:

> If one has knowledge [*gnosis*], he is from above. If he is called, he hears, he answers, and he turns to him who is calling him and ascends to him. And he knows in what manner he is called. Having knowledge, he does the will of the one who called him, he wishes to be pleasing to him... He who is to have knowledge in this manner knows where he comes from and where he is going. He knows as one who having become drunk has turned away from his drunkenness and having returned to himself, has set right what are his own.[34]

Another Gnostic tract, the Excerpta de Theodoto, states:

> What makes us free is the gnosis
> of who we were
> of what we have become
> of where we were
> of wherein we have been cast
> of whereto we are hastening
> of what we are being freed
> of what birth really is
> of what rebirth really is.[35]

The Gospel of Philip is more direct still: 'Ignorance is a slave. Knowledge [*gnosis*] is freedom. If we know the truth, we shall find the fruits of the truth within us. If we are joined to it, it will bring fulfilment.'[36]

What differentiates Gnosticism from mainstream Christianity is the idea that *gnosis* alone will save, as opposed to faith. The Catholic Church adds the caveat of receiving the sacraments in addition to faith, while Protestantism stresses the vital importance of good works. The Gnostics will hear none of that, stressing that one is only saved through what goes on within one's heart and soul. For the Gnostic, faith is a poor cousin to *gnosis* as it effectively implies a distance between the believer and the divine. As the Gnostic bishop Stephan Hoeller noted:

> William James... remarked that to most people faith means having faith in someone else's faith. In the minds of many religious folk, faith has thus devolved into a belief received second-hand from other believers, none of whom are likely to have had any experience of the object of their faith.[37]

How, then, does one achieve *gnosis*, that spontaneous awakening which permanently shifts one's consciousness? It can come unbidden at any time, through ordinarily normal activities such as listening to a piece of music, seeing a particular landscape at a certain time of day, or experiencing a sudden moment of clarity and silence into which something else makes its presence known. Alternatively, it can be achieved through the medium of a teacher and by participating in rituals, or it can be a mixture of all of these things. Until the discovery of the Nag Hammadi library, it was generally assumed that the Gnostics had very little in the way of ritual and sacraments, but texts such as the Gospel of Philip indicate that this was not so. We shall examine this element of Gnosticism later.

Dualism

The Gnostic world view is decidedly dualistic in character. The Church Fathers – ever the effective propagandists – portrayed the Gnostics as world-haters. Needless to say, this was typical Church-sponsored character assassination and the truth of the matter is much more subtle.

Dualism existed before Christianity and may even be older than recorded history itself. The term was first coined in 1700 by the English Orientalist, Thomas Hyde, to describe any religious system which held that God and the devil were two opposing, coeternal principles.[38] The meaning of the term evolved to include any system that revolved around a central, binary pairing (such as the mind/body split in the philosophy of Descartes, or the immortal soul/mortal body from that of Plato). Dualist strands exist in one form or another in all major religions, whether monotheistic (acknowledging one god, such as Islam, Judaism and Christianity), polytheistic (acknowledging many gods, such as Shintoism, some forms of Wicca or the pantheon of classical Greece), or monistic (acknowledging that everything – the Divine, matter and humanity – is of one and the same essential substance, such as certain schools of Hinduism, Buddhism, Taoism and Pantheism). For example, fundamentalist Christianity has a pronounced dualist slant in that it sees many things in the world – rock music, drugs, New Age philosophies, Hollywood blockbusters – as being the work of the devil. Likewise, extremist Islamic groups see non-Muslims as either essentially asleep to the truth, or actively engaged in undermining the religion of the Prophet. In both cases, an 'us and them' mentality prevails, from which there is only one escape route (belief in Jesus and the Prophet Muhammad respectively).

Despite these varying levels of dualism in the different faiths of the world, religious dualism proper stands apart in positing the notion of the two opposing principles of good and evil. Within the dualist tradition itself, there are generally held to be two schools of thought: absolute, or radical, dualism, and mitigated, or monarchian, dualism. The Italian historian of religions, Ugo Bianchi, identified three distinct features of dualism:

1. Absolute, or radical, dualism regards the two principles of good and evil as coeternal and equal, whereas mitigated dualism

regards the evil principle as a secondary, lesser power to the good principle.

2. Absolute dualism sees the two principles as locked in combat for all eternity and, in many schools, regards time as cyclical (these dualist traditions, therefore, tend to believe in reincarnation), while mitigated dualism sees historical time as being finite; at the end of time, the evil principle will be defeated by the good.

3. Absolute dualism sees the material world as intrinsically evil, but mitigated dualism regards creation as essentially good.[39]

Given these parameters, Gnosticism could be regarded as mitigated dualism, in that it sees matter and evil as the creation of a lesser god, the Demiurge. This does not necessarily mean that Gnostics see the world as evil, although it is quite possible that some of the more ascetic Gnostics of antiquity may have subscribed to this view. Rather, the Gnostic view acknowledges that the world is imperfect, but that those imperfections should not blind us to the presence of good, both within ourselves and in the world around us. Indeed, that there is goodness in the world at all is a sign that we can be saved. This idea is inextricably linked with Gnostic creation myths.

Gnostic Creation Myths

This is where things traditionally get a little complicated, as there is a seemingly bewildering array of Gnostic creation myths. The Church Fathers made much of this, declaring that Gnosticism was a confused mass of fabulous fictions and downright madness; needless to say, this was yet another instance of the Church misinterpreting what the Gnostics were trying to do. For the Gnostics, myth and creativity were highly valued, as they revealed deeper truths than those of history or dogma. Their creation myths therefore are diverse, so what follows is necessarily something of a simplified generalisation.

As we have noted, the Gnostics posited the existence of two gods, the incompetent, arrogant creator God, the Demiurge, and the true God who exists beyond all created matter and possible attempts to describe what the true God actually is. The Demiurge is often identified with the God of the Old Testament, but is not usually seen as evil. His main failing is his arrogance; he believes that there are no other gods but him. The epithet 'creator God' is in fact slightly misleading, as most Gnostic creation stories depict the *actual* creator of matter as Sophia, the wisdom of the true God. The Demiurge is merely the bigheaded, boisterous artisan who fashioned matter into the forms of the created world.

Before time and space began, the true God existed in a realm known as the Pleroma, which means fullness, together with a female divine principle, known as Ennoia, or Thought. The true God does not create, but rather emanates, which is to say that things come forth from him. In other words, rather than the true God saying 'Let there be light', as the God of the Old Testament does, light comes forth from the true God as if it were breath; it is not deliberate, willed creation. A series of emanations resulted in the creation of a number of divine figures known as aeons. Central to the idea of emanation is that each successive emanation is somewhat lesser than that from which it emanated, like the ripples on the surface of a pond after a stone has been dropped into the middle of it, with the ripples in the centre of the pond being closer to the stone than the ones at the pond's edge. Sophia, the Wisdom of God, being the youngest of the aeons, is also therefore the furthest from God, and it was through her desire to know the true God that an emanation came forth from her without the knowledge or participation of her male consort (all the aeons having partners). This emanation produced the dark chaos which was to become matter, but at this stage was a soulless place, ' limitless darkness and bottomless water'.[40] Gnostic texts describe it as an abortion. Sophia, being disturbed by the darkness, decided to create a being to rule over it and breathed life into an androgynous, lion-faced being known as Ialdabaoth, a word which could mean either 'begetter of the heavenly powers' (i.e., 'creator of the world') or 'childish god'.

Ialdabaoth is none other than the Demiurge, who is ignorant even of his own mother. Sophia tries to explain to him that there are powers greater than he, but he will not listen and begins to create heaven and earth out of the matter over which he is the chief archon (the word is derived from the Greek for 'petty official'). Amongst Ialdabaoth's first creations are other archons, each ruling over the seven heavens that Ialdabaoth creates for them, all of which exist below the realm of Sophia, who dwells in the eighth heaven. The furthest realm from the Demiurge's creation – so far removed as to be indescribable – is that of the true God.

Ialdabaoth and his archons spend a lot of time squabbling and fighting amongst themselves, the Gnostic version of the 'War in Heaven' that causes the fall of Lucifer in orthodox Christian legend. At length, Ialdabaoth declares that 'There is no other God but me', thus directly linking him with the God of the Old Testament, who also declares approximately the same thing. Sophia hears this and calls out to him, 'You are mistaken, Samael!' (The name means 'blind god'.) Ialdabaoth demands that if there is a higher power than himself, that power must make itself known to him. Light then descends from the higher realms, in which he can discern a human form, and Ialdabaoth is ashamed. This figure is the so-called Adam of Light, who remains with Ialdabaoth for a short time before returning from whence he came. Ialdabaoth, ever the jealous god, eventually decides to create his own version of Adam with the help of the archons, but lacks the ability to give him a soul. As Sophia breathed life into Ialdabaoth, so she breathes soul into Adam, and this takes us up to the story of Adam and Eve.

The Biblical story of the Garden of Eden tells us that God creates Adam out of the dust and breathes life into him. Later, while Adam is slumbering in a deep sleep, God takes one of Adam's ribs and fashions out of it the first woman, Eve, who is to be Adam's wife in Eden. Adam and Eve then live in a paradisical state until the Serpent – often identified with the devil – tempts Eve to eat the forbidden fruit of the tree of knowledge. This Satanic spanner in the divine works appears to scupper God's plan as the original state of harmony is shattered: the first couple have their eyes opened to good and evil and became aware of their nakedness, which causes them shame. God discovers this one day while walking in the Garden and banishes them. In the first of his fits of Old Testament anger, he also afflicts them with mutual enmity, and tells Eve that childbirth will bring her pain and that she will be subservient to her husband. For his part, Adam is cursed to return to the ground and to earn his keep by the sweat of his brow all the days of his life.

The Gnostics would not have disagreed with the actual series of events, save of course pointing out that it was Sophia who breathed life into Adam, not the Old Testament's belligerent God. Where they differ from the orthodox is in their interpretation of Eve and the Serpent, and also in their reading of the story not as history, but as myth. For the Gnostics, the Serpent is the wisest of all creatures (some accounts have him being guided by the wisdom of Sophia), whose urging of Eve to eat of the tree of knowledge does not cause the Fall of mankind, but its awakening. What Adam and Eve have gained is *gnosis*, which makes them aware that the true God is not the deity who banished them from Eden. Furthermore, as Eve was the first human to gain *gnosis*, Gnostic texts generally paint her as being superior to Adam. Some, such as the Nag Hammadi text known as On the Origin of the World, describe her as being the daughter and messenger of Sophia sent to waken her sleeping partner.

The Gnostics had a fondness for myth and allegory, and they would have interpreted Adam and Eve, not as the first humans whose actual physical existence is proven by the Book of Genesis, but rather as aspects of our psychological and spiritual make-up. Adam represents the soul, traditionally seen as the domain of mind and emotions, while Eve represents spirit, the higher consciousness that is aware of its divine origins. With this in mind, we can now see that the story of the Garden of Eden shows the higher part of the human spirit (Eve) awakening the lower part (Adam) to *gnosis*; the complete person (Eve and Adam together as an androgynous whole) is then able to start the long journey back to the divine realms above the seven heavens where the true God and the aeons reside.

Why did the Gnostics favour myth and allegory? An educated guess would attribute this tendency to the intellectual and philosophical climate of the first centuries of the Common Era, in which myth and allegory flourished. The ideas of Plato and his followers dominated the thought of the Hellenistic world in which Gnosticism first flourished and the stories they told in order to express their ideas were understood as allegory, not history. For instance, no one would have regarded the famous story of Plato's cave as actual history. Rather, it was seen for what it was: an allegory of the human situation that never took place in historical reality, but rather continued to be relevant because of its timeless, almost mythic element. The story is incidentally also rather Gnostic in its view of the world and it is perhaps worth stopping for a moment to reacquaint ourselves with it.

Some prisoners have been held in a cave since childhood. They are all chained in such a manner as they can only stare straight ahead at the cave wall. A fire burns in the centre of the cave behind them, which casts shadows onto the walls. The shadows they can see are cast by various animals and plants that the jailers carry along a raised walkway on the other side of the fire. The prisoners play a game, naming the shadows, and when the jailers respond, the prisoners believe it is actually the shadows who are speaking. The prisoners, being unable to move or turn around, mistake the shadows and the voices for the only reality. What would happen, asks Plato, if one of the prisoners was forced to stand up and turn around? He would be blinded by the fire, which he would at first take to be less real than the shadows to which he's been accustomed for so long. And what if then the hapless prisoner were to be taken outside the cave altogether? The sunlight would have an even greater disorienting effect upon him. Eventually, once the prisoner has realised the enormity of what he has experienced, he will understand that the world he has lived in for so long was unreal, with the greater, true reality being above and beyond him. It is a reality to which he can gain access, but first he must be freed from his confinement.

This mythic sensibility, which enabled the Gnostics to understand Plato, would have almost certainly informed their way of reading the Old Testament as well. Stories, the Gnostics understood – even Biblical ones – do not have to have actually *happened* in order for them to have profound meaning for us all. As the Gospel of Philip acknowledges, the truths of *gnosis* have to be transformed into poetic and mythic language in order for us to understand them:

> Truth didn't come into the world naked
> but in types and images. Truth is received only
> that way. There is rebirth and its image.
> They must be reborn through image.[41]

The Gnostic World View

The existence of evil in the world has long perplexed philosophers and the religious. The orthodox Christian view is that evil exists because of human error. Eve, in other words, is to blame, which coincidentally says much about the rampant institutional misogyny that has existed in mainstream Christianity since the first century. Eve's transgression cast a long shadow over humanity, so the orthodox view claims, a shadow which was only cleared by the sacrificial mission of Christ. As we have seen, the Gnostics hold Eve in high regard and view the nature of Christ's mission in rather different terms to that of the Church as well. And, as might be expected, they have an explanation for the existence of evil in the world that is at odds with the Church's teachings.

Evil is in the world, according to the Gnostic view, quite simply because it was created by Ialdabaoth, a 'malicious grudger' according to one Gnostic text.[42] The Demiurge is usually seen by the Gnostics more as a minor deity given to all too human outbursts rather than actually being evil. Ialdabaoth's arrogance and jealousy cause him to spend most of the Old Testament stamping around like a playground bully, dishing out plagues and tempests whenever humanity displeases him (which is often). As the true God does not create, neither does he intervene directly, thus allowing evil to permeate the Demiurge's flawed creation.

In Terry Gilliam's *Time Bandits*, a piece of evil appears at the end of the film, looking very much like a piece of smoking charcoal. While Gnostic and non-Gnostic alike may find this amusing, the Gnostic interpretation of what evil actually is may differ from the more orthodox definitions. Rather than seeing evil as being the work of the devil, most Gnostics would agree that it is generally the product of ignorance: people do bad things simply because 'they know not what they do',[43] nor how much harm they do themselves when they harm another.

A more esoteric interpretation defines evil as 'darkened matter', in the sense that matter is a darkening of the original divine substance: with each successive emanation, so matter at once became more concrete, less divine and, at the same time, also less good. Thus there is a strong link for the Gnostic between matter and evil, although the actual evilness of matter itself is open to dispute. The modern Gnostic Stephan Hoeller defines matter as evil only insofar as it has a tendency to distract the soul from its primary purpose, that of undertaking the journey back to its divine origins beyond the created world, or, what is worse, making it forget completely that while it is in the world, it is not of it.

Lest this sounds a little gloomy – and the Gnostics were frequently accused of being pessimists – we should remind ourselves that being in the world, while it might be compared to a prison, or to poverty, is ultimately hopeful in that everyone is said to possess a spark of the divine within them. One of the results of gaining *gnosis* is that one also gains knowledge of this spark, and with it the realisation that part of the true God is within us, that we are part of the true God. Once we come to realise our true nature, we long to go home, or, at the very least, willingly endure the exile of this world, knowing that there is a better one to come. However, Ialdabaoth and his archons lie in wait everywhere to keep people ignorant of their true nature and to keep them in thrall to the passions, the pleasures of the flesh and the pursuit of worldly wealth and power.

While all Gnostics saw the world as both an exile and a prison, they also saw this divine drama being played out in a world that essentially cohered to the classical model. This was a geocentric view of creation, in which the world sat within the seven spheres of the Moon, Venus, Mercury, the Sun, Mars, Jupiter and Saturn. These spheres were all under the control of the archons, with the eighth sphere either being seen as Ialdabaoth's domain, or sometimes as the lowest (i.e., most material) part of the Pleroma, the rest of which lay far above and beyond the spheres of material existence.

In adapting the classical model of the world – adding extra spheres above the traditional seven – the Gnostics were conforming to what would become standard practice (if anything in Gnosticism could said to be 'standard practice'). They likewise took an interest in astrology, perhaps part of the putative Iranian influence on Gnosticism, as Babylon was seen as the cradle of the astrologer's art. The heavens were reinterpreted along Gnostic lines, with archonic influences working alongside the traditional planetary ones.

The Gnostics had a linear view of time, but some also believed in reincarnation. Some Gnostic texts, such as the Book of Jeu, are instructions for the soul after it has left the body; Western equivalents to the Tibetan Book of the Dead. If, however, the soul is prevented from returning to the Pleroma by the archons, it is reincarnated. Some Gnostics believed that when all of the souls or divine sparks have returned to the Pleroma, the domain of the archons – the created universe – will come to an end. Indeed, some held that matter had been created expressly to trap particles of the divine.

Moving throughout this world was the power of Sophia, always ready to help the seeker on his or her journey. All the Gnostic schools and groups held her in high regard, and it is to these schools that we now turn.

Teachers and Traditions

During the first four centuries after Christ, what was to become the official Church was a diverse collection of churches and communities that did not form a coherent whole, which led to Church Fathers such as Irenaeus spending a great deal of time trying to get Christian communities to toe what would become the party line in matters of belief and practice. The Gnostics, however, did not have an Irenaeus of their own; indeed, they would have opposed the whole notion of one set of beliefs and practices that were suitable for everybody. The way to *gnosis* was always a personal journey, which meant that scripture and practice would differ from group to group, or from person to person. It was long thought that Gnosticism was not much more than a philosophy, with little in the way of actual practice and sacrament, a view ably reinforced by the likes of Irenaeus and his fulminating colleagues. However, since the discovery of the Nag Hammadi texts, it now appears that the Gnostics did indeed have rituals and sacraments that they practised.

In this chapter, we will examine some of the more well-known of the Gnostic groups and their charismatic teachers, and in the chapter following, the two full-blown religions that developed from the Gnostic seedbed.

First-Century Gnostic Teachers

The first Gnostic teacher whose name has come down to us is

Simon the Magician, who is more commonly known by his Latin name, Simon Magus. He hailed from Samaria, a region known for its heterodox Judaism and, according to Justin Martyr, was apparently active during the reign of the Emperor Claudius. This early date – 41–54 CE – makes Simon a contemporary of the surviving Apostles and also St Paul. It is therefore not surprising to find Simon mentioned in the Acts of the Apostles, where, as we have already noted, Simon comes into conflict with the Apostles Peter and John and also later engages in magical battles with Peter in the apocryphal Acts of Peter. Interestingly, although Simon repents of his magic in Acts 8.24, the Church Fathers continued to regard him as an arch-heretic for centuries after his time; perhaps they knew that the portrayal of Simon's repentance in Acts was a fabrication written to make the Apostles seem all-victorious, or perhaps they had had first-hand encounters with Simonian Gnostics and realised that Simon's teachings still had a following.

Simon is traditionally held to have been a disciple of John the Baptist, or of John's pupil Dositheus. Like the orthodox therefore, the Gnostics could – and did – claim that their tradition stretched back to the time of Jesus and was therefore as valid, if not more so, than the teachings of the Roman Church. Simon is said to have written a number of books, amongst which were *The Four Quarters of the World* and *The Sermons of the Refuter*. Although both are sadly lost to us, we know that the latter volume made out the God of the Old Testament to be a sham, while the Serpent in the Garden of Eden was portrayed as a wise teacher. A third tract, the *Apophasis Megalê* (meaning 'Great Pronouncement' or 'Great Exposition'), survives only in fragments.[44] The text is generally thought to have been written after Simon's death by one or more of his students. What most memorably survives of Simon's teaching, however, is inextricably bound up with his relationship with his partner, Helen.

Like Mary Magdalene, Helen was depicted as a prostitute.

Although many scholars of early Christianity now view the Magdalene-as-whore story as a very effective piece of Church-sponsored character assassination, with Helen, we are on less certain terrain. So little is actually known about her that she will forever remain in the realms of myth; given the Gnostic predilection for mythological truths, this is perhaps fitting. Simon is said to have encountered Helen in a brothel in Tyre, where he recognised her as an embodiment of Sophia. This story is of uncertain provenance and may have been fabricated by the Church Fathers to discredit Simon and his teaching. What we do know, from Irenaeus, is that Simon taught the existence of an ultimate, pre-existent God, whose first emanation, the Ennoia (Thought) was feminine. The Ennoia becomes God's partner and follows his divine plan by creating angels and archangels. In a variation on the War in Heaven idea, in Simon's cosmology there is a Mutiny in Heaven, with some of the angelic orders turning against the Ennoia. She is imprisoned, subjected to every degradation, finally being forced to incarnate in the world, trapped in a woman's body. She journeys through a number of incarnations, being at one time Helen of Troy, before finally washing up as a prostitute in Tyre, at which point the pre-existent God sends an avatar of himself into the world to rescue her. According to his detractors, Simon saw himself as this avatar, but this may again be the Church Fathers up to their old tricks; at the very least, the story is perhaps the earliest Sophia prototype we have and can be seen as a lament for the soul's fall into ignorance.

The Simonian school continued through his pupil, Menander, and his pupil, Saturninus. Menander (d. *c.* 80 CE), like Simon, had a reputation for being a magician, which may be another way of saying that he taught salvation by *gnosis*. Saturninus appears to have been an ascetic, who taught the existence of the Unknown God existing above and beyond the created universe. The world, according to Saturninus, was created by lesser powers, who also created man. When they did so, they entrapped fragments of the divine light in each person, a light which would be freed by the arrival of a saviour, who would come in human form and bestow the liberation of *gnosis*.

Another early teacher was Cerinthus, who was active around the late first century CE and into the early part of the second. He was said to have been a contemporary of St John, who detested Cerinthus and his teaching with a pássion. One day, according to Irenaeus, St John went to the public baths in Ephesus. To his horror, Cerinthus was bathing inside and St John fled, exclaiming 'Let us flee, lest the bath house fall down; because Cerinthus, the enemy of truth, is inside.'[45] Irenaeus believed that St John was the author of the gospel bearing his name, which was presumably written to counter Cerinthus's Christ, who was not divine but very much a mortal man whose divine nature entered him at his baptism, then left him again at the crucifixion. The mortal Jesus will only rise from the dead on the last day, together with all of humanity. John's Jesus, by contrast, is divine from birth and bodily ascends to heaven at the end of this earthly ministry.

Basilides

The second century CE saw Gnosticism flourish. The first great teacher to emerge during this period was Basilides, who was active in Alexandria during the reigns of the Roman Emperors Hadrian and Antoninus Pius (117–61 CE). Basilides is important because he saw himself as both a Christian Gnostic and a theologian. His Christ, therefore, was Gnostic. According to tradition, he is said to have studied under Glaucias, who was one of St Peter's disciples, and possibly also under Menander and Saturninus. Evidently something of a mystic who required serious disciples to begin their training by observing a five-year silence, little of Basilides' teaching has survived directly. As with many other Gnostic teachers therefore, we are almost entirely dependent upon what the Church Fathers had to say about him. Surprisingly, they do not agree, which suggests that Irenaeus and Hippolytus – authors of the two best accounts of Basilides – either got their facts muddled, or they failed to grasp the subtleties of Basilides' thought. Irenaeus paints Basilides as a radical dualist, while Hippolytus sees him as a monistic thinker, heavily influenced by Greek philosophy.

Basilides, according to Irenaeus, taught the existence of the unknown true God, from whom the angelic orders emanate. Originally there were just six: mind, Christ, the word, prudence, wisdom and power. From these came 365 further angelic powers, each creating a heaven of their own. As with all emanatory cosmologies, the succeeding heavens are lower and more material than the emanation from which they came. The last and lowest of the 365 angelic powers created the material world and men, who are ruled by a god called Abraxas, identified with the God of the Old Testament. The true God then sent Christ into the world to bring the liberating *gnosis*, but he escaped crucifixion by getting Simon of Cyrene to stand in for him on Calvary. In Hippolytus's account, the true God emanated a 'world-seed', out of which everything came. Unusually, these emanations move upwards towards God (usually the reverse is true, with successive emanations moving away from God in a downwards direction). The emanation is described as being comprised of three 'Sonships', the first and lightest of which is able to rejoin the true God, the second requires the help of the Holy Spirit, while the third remains trapped in matter. This third 'Sonship' is the divine spark in every soul, whose worldly exile can be brought to an end via the redeeming message of Christ, whose mission it is to gather the Third Sonship together and take it home.

Marcion

Basilides' teachings seem not to have travelled much further than Egypt. The same cannot be said for the work of Marcion. Indeed, the nascent Church regarded him and his teachings as the biggest threat they had faced up to that time and Marcion is still regarded by the Catholic Church as one of the greatest of the heresiarchs.

Marcion was born in Pontus, a port on the Black Sea, around the turn of the first century. He was raised in a Christian family; his father was either a priest or bishop and was also a ship owner. Marcion followed in his father's footsteps, becoming both a priest and a wealthy businessman. He was in Rome by around 140 CE, where he was a substantial donor to the Church. His attempts to win the Church round to his way of thinking ended in failure, and in July 144 he founded his own rival church. The Church, not wishing to sully its coffers with heretical funds, returned his donation.

Marcion taught the existence of the two gods, calling the incompetent creator God the God of the Law, and the true god the Good God. Jesus came to save mankind, but did not inhabit an actual physical body – an heretical position which became known as Docetism. The only true scriptures were the Sermon on the Mount – especially the Beatitudes – and an edited version of the Gospel of Luke, with its Jewish elements removed.[46] Marcion believed that the Church's adoption of the Old Testament and its jealous god was merely a ploy to gain Jewish converts to Christianity and sought to establish a Christianity that was entirely free from its Jewish origins. The only person who had understood Christ's mission correctly was St Paul and therefore the Pauline letters were also incorporated into Marcion's reduced canon.[47] It is possible that Marcion's attempts to draw up an official Christian canon may have eventually led to the Church forming its own, which was done at the Council of Nicaea in 325. By this time, there were Marcionite churches all over the

Graeco-Roman world; declared heretical, Marcionism finally died out in the fifth century.

Although Marcion believed in the two gods and also held certain other views in common with Gnosticism – such as asceticism and the flesh being evil – precisely how Gnostic he was remains in dispute. Perhaps crucially, there is no liberating *gnosis* in Marcion, no divine spark within and no mythological cosmologies and cosmogonies. Marcion would have probably seen himself as a Church reformer rather than as a Gnostic, but his many adversaries within the Church did not agree and frequently grouped him together with other Gnostics in their diatribes against what they saw as pernicious attempts to undermine the one true church. However, in attempting to establish a 'pure' form of Christianity based around the teachings of the 'real' Jesus, Marcion lit a fire that has never been completely extinguished; many writers and theologians today concern themselves with just such issues. This is perhaps Marcion's greatest legacy.

Valentinus

Valentinus (*c.* 100–*c.* 160/180) was the greatest of the second-century Gnostics and was, after Marcion, the Church's biggest enemy of the time. Indeed, in some cases, Valentinus and his followers were regarded as a more insidious threat to the Church than Marcion, because they were harder to detect. Unlike Marcion, Valentinus tried to make Gnosticism compatible with the Church and developed a complex form of Gnosticism that incorporated an immense mythology intended to 'embrace everything... external and internal'.[48] Thus Valentinus and his followers regarded themselves as Christians and most definitely part of the Christian community. They attended 'mainstream' churches and also met together on their own, a fact which, as we shall see, did not escape the ever-watchful eyes of the Church Fathers.

Valentinus was born in Egypt around the turn of the first century CE and was educated in Alexandria, where Basilides was teaching at the time (although we don't know for sure if the two ever met). Around 135, Valentinus moved to Rome, remaining there for around 25 years. Marcion was also active there during this era, but again, we don't know whether Valentinus came into contact with him. Valentinus's disciples, however, maintained that, during his early years in Rome, Valentinus had studied with Theudas, a disciple of St Paul. What little we do know of Valentinus' life suggests that he was a widely respected member of the Church and, according to Tertullian, almost became pope but lost out to Pius I, who became pontiff around 140.[49] After this defeat, Valentinus is said to have been denounced as a heretic, but continued to teach in Rome for another 20 years. He then either died, or, according to the Church Father Epiphanius, went to Cyprus; this version of events has him teaching there well into old age. However, Valentinus does not appear to have been universally regarded as a heretic during his lifetime and may have been an influence on the Church Father Origen, who, of all the Fathers, seems to have been one of the very few who was sympathetic to Gnosticism.

Valentinus and his followers created the most fully developed Gnostic system, in which Greek, Oriental and Christian ideas mix to produce the closest Gnosticism comes to establishing its own 'orthodoxy'. Such an idea is, as we have noted, anathema to the Gnostics; many of Valentinus' disciples added to his work and claimed to have 'improved the master'. The Fathers, as usual, railed against this, failing to see that Gnosticism is a personal, creative experience in which the truth continues to expand and adapt, according to the abilities – both receptive and creative – of the recipient.

Although Valentinus' system is the most developed form of Gnosticism, it is not possible to reconstruct it exactly, due to a lack of primary sources. Valentinus' own writings have largely not survived, except for the fragments quoted by the Fathers and the Nag Hammadi text, the Gospel of Truth. What we can say is therefore somewhat speculative, although he appears to have been influenced by Greek and Oriental ideas and mixed them with Christian concepts in what appears to have been an attempt to provide a comprehensive system that would serve for all Christians, Gnostic or otherwise. As with other Gnostic cosmologies, Valentinus posits the existence of a pre-existent, unknown God, who resides in the Pleroma, undisturbed and unmanifest. A series of aeons ultimately emanates, forming 15 male–female pairs, reflecting the unknown God, who is said to be dyadic (a father–mother). The most important are the first four pairs, Bythos ('primal depth' the male principle) and Ennoia ('thought', also called Charis, meaning 'grace' and Sigē, meaning 'silence', who is feminine); Nous ('understanding', male) and Alētheia ('truth', female), then Logos ('the Word', male) and Zoë ('life', female); and finally Anthropos ('man', male) and Ekklesia ('church', female). The emanations continue, right down to the last who, as in other systems, is Sophia ('wisdom', female). At the border of the Pleroma is Horos ('the Limit'), within which the aeons happily resided until the creation of the Kenoma ('Lower World', also known as the Deficiency).

The aeons long to know their creator and Sophia undertakes this mission on her own, without the knowledge of her consort, which results in the appearance of 'ignorance', which in turn ultimately leads to the emanation of matter, the Demiurge and the material world. Reflecting Plato's idea of the World of Forms, which holds that everything in the material world is but a poor reflection of the Ideal World above it, so Valentinus' system posits that the material world is a shadowy, flawed version of the Pleroma, the two worlds sometimes being referred to as the Hebdomad (from *hebdomas*, meaning 'seven', a reference to the seven spheres of the material world) and Ogdoad (from *ogdoas*, meaning 'eight', referring to the eighth heaven), respectively. At some point during or immediately prior to the creation of the Hebdomad, Sophia is split in two, with her higher self being stopped at the Limit and returning into the Pleroma, while her lower self breaks through and afterwards remains trapped in matter. It is this lower Sophia who brings forth the Demiurge. A fresh pair of aeons, 'Christ' and 'Holy Spirit', are sent into the material world in order to rescue her.

The Valentinian system regards mankind as the work of the Demiurge, who rules over the Hebdomad. There are three main groups of humans: hylics, psychics and pneumatics. Hylics are people who are resolutely 'in matter' and care only for the concerns of the flesh: attaining pleasure and comfort, avoiding pain and unnecessary thought. The psychics are people who are not so caught up in the pleasures and pains of earthly existence, but who are more inclined to thinking, feeling and participating in exoteric (i.e., dogmatic) religion. The pneumatics are spiritually aware people, who are above dogma and division, and who are able to receive *gnosis*. In dividing humanity up like this, Valentinus is reflecting the Gnostic tendency towards elitism, for which they were frequently criticised by the Church Fathers. (Needless to say, the Fathers themselves were somewhat elitist, in adopting a stance in which they claimed to be the One True Church above all others, Gnostic or otherwise.)

In defence of Valentinus, though, the reason he delineated people into these three groups was due to how he thought they would respond to the message of Christ, which, as in all Gnosticism, is one of liberating *gnosis*, rather than the sacrificial redemption of main-stream Christianity. In the case of the hylics, the spiritual seed 'falls on the path', in other words goes unnoticed, while in the case of the psychics, they perhaps hear the message, but are too caught up in intellectualising the whole concept of salvation and possibly retreat into the iron arms of dogma. It is only the pneumatics who are able to hear the liberating words of Jesus and *actually understand* what they mean. Pneumatics, therefore, are Gnostics and can progress on the path back to the Pleroma.

Despite this apparent elitism, however, Valentinus' philosophy holds that anyone can attain *gnosis*, even if he or she had originally been a hylic or a psychic. Indeed, the more people who attain *gnosis*, the more it heals the rift between the Ogdoad and the Hebdomad. In other words, in Valentinianism, attaining *gnosis* not only liberates oneself, but also helps to restore the material world to the unblemished state of the Pleroma; individual salvation is therefore intimately linked to the salvation of the whole.

Valentinus' Christology is rather confused, which could be the result of a lack of original sources, the distortions of the Church Fathers and the elaborations of successive generations of Valentinians themselves. As Valentinus' system holds that the material world is an inferior copy of the Pleroma, so there are two Christs, a heavenly one and his earthly copy, who did not have a body of flesh and blood, but only the appearance of one, and who also did not suffer on the cross. (Like Marcion, Valentinus was a Docetic.) Debates about the nature of Christ's person raged in the Church for centuries, and so it was with the Valentinians: the Italian school argued that Christ only became pneumatic – endowed with the wisdom of Sophia – at his baptism, while the Anatolian school (scattered across Syria and Egypt) maintained that Christ had a pneumatic body from birth. Unlike the mainstream church, differences of opinion amongst the Gnostics did not lead to persecution and bloodshed; indeed, lack of agreement was seen as natural and theological diversity was encouraged.

Aside from the two differing schools of thought within Valentinianism, Valentinus had a number of successors, perhaps the most noteworthy of whom were Ptolemaeus and Heracleon. They both belonged to the Italian school and lived in the second half of the second century. In Ptolemaeus's hands, Valentinian Gnosticism becomes a system concerned primarily with the fate of the psychics; it is essentially for their liberation that Christ came. For Heracleon, the core of Gnosticism was salvation and, as a consequence, he was less inclined to create myths about the aeons and the fall of Sophia. A third Valentinian, Marcus, seemed to have practised a form of Gnosticism that bore similarities with the Greek mystery cults and developed a mythology that involved gematria and mystical speculation about letters of the alphabet, which had long been practised by Pythagoras and his followers, and later by Kabbalistic Jews. Marcus seems to have particularly irked the Church Fathers, who denounced him as a devil-worshipper and idolater; due to the unfortunate loss of original sources, we don't know how Marcus regarded the Church Fathers, but we can assume that the feeling was probably mutual.

Later Gnostics

There are several other second-century teachers of note. One, Monoimus, lived in the latter part of the second century and, like the Valentinian Marcus, developed a form of Gnosticism that incorporated number mysticism and geometry. He also advised a friend in a letter how to find the true God, which is worth quoting in full, as it provides a refreshingly simple example of Gnostic writing in contrast with some of their complex mythologies:

Cease to seek after God in created things, such as the universe and its like; seek Him within thyself, and learn who it is, who includes always all things within himself, saying: 'My God, my mind, my reason, my soul, my body.' And learn from where comes sorrow and joy, and love and hate, and being awake against one's will, and sleeping against one's will, and falling in love against one's will. And if thou shouldst closely inquire about this, thou wilt find Him in thyself, one and many, like the atom; thus thou wilt find by way of thyself a way out of thyself. [50]

Bardaisan (155–233), a Syrian nobleman philosopher, acted as spiritual adviser to King Abgar IX of Edessa. Interest in spiritual matters seems to have run in the family, as one of Abgar's predecessors, Abgar V, was said to have written to Jesus requesting a cure for an illness that he was afflicted with at the time. Jesus wrote back, declining to go, but instead sent a cloth upon which was either a miraculous painted image of Jesus, or in some versions of the story, a cloth that had the imprint of his face on it. Needless to say, the image had healing properties and Abgar made a full recovery.

Bardaisan's own achievements at the court of Abgar IX were just as remarkable in their own way. He invented the genre of the Christian hymn and composed a substantial body of them, numbering around 150; his work was later plagiarised by the Church Father Ephraim of Edessa, who claimed them as his own compositions while denouncing their real author as a heretic. Bardaisan also wrote a number of treatises, the only surviving one being *The Book of the Laws of Countries*, which was discovered in the nineteenth century. A quite widely circulated Gnostic text, the Hymn of the Pearl, is also thought to have been Bardaisan's work. Perhaps Bardaisan's greatest achievement, though, was in converting King Abgar to Gnosticism; under his reign, Edessa became the only Gnostic state in history.

'Libertine' Gnostics

Certain Gnostic schools were portrayed by the Church Fathers as libertines of monstrous proportions, murderers and thieves who idolised Judas Iscariot and committed every sin imaginable. To this group belong the Carpocratians, Cainites and Borborites. Needless to say, the Fathers either misunderstood these Gnostics, or deliberately exaggerated and distorted what these groups were practising. The Carpocratian school was founded by Carpocrates, who lived in Alexandria around the turn of the first century CE. A contemporary of Basilides, Carpocrates taught with his wife Alexandra, a fact which, as might be expected, did not sit too well with the Church Fathers. Their Gnosticism was influenced by Plato, with the Pleroma being equivalent to the Platonic higher world of ideal forms. They also taught reincarnation and believed that, in order to be liberated from the material world and its archons, a person had to experience all that life has to offer; saturated with experience, the person eventually tires of earthly existence and longs to return to the Pleroma. This process could happen over the course of many lifetimes, or just one. For Irenaeus, this meant that the Carpocratians indulged in every vice and crime there was, as such deeds were a prerequisite of the spiritual path, although he doubted that they practised what they preached. Indeed, there is no evidence of Gnostics – Carpocratians or otherwise – ever indulging in immoral or licentious behaviour. The same, sadly, cannot be said for the Church.

The Cainites, who originated around the same time as the Carpocratians, venerated the Old Testament figure of Cain, the first murderer. Cain's murder of his brother Abel was an act that was motivated by anger and jealousy: according to the fourth chapter of Genesis, both brothers make sacrificial offerings to God (the Demiurge), but the so-called Almighty inexplicably rejects Cain's offering while accepting Abel's. In killing Abel, Cain is rebelling against the inferior creator God and all his works. The Cainites' other most revered figure was Judas Iscariot, whose betrayal of Christ was not seen as it usually is, as the foulest treachery in history, but as something actually sanctioned by Jesus himself, as it allowed him to return to the Pleroma when his earthly ministry was complete. The Gospel of Judas, which recounts this version of events and also portrays Judas as Christ's most enlightened disciple, was the Cainites' principal text. (We shall examine this gospel further in a later chapter.) Like the Carpocratians, the Cainites held that one has to pass through all experiences in order to be liberated from them. And again, as with the Carpocratians, although the Cainites espoused antinomian views, no evidence has come down to us that suggests they behaved illegally or immorally. Both groups were instead victims of the Church Fathers' rumour-mongering, a campaign which was so successful that both groups became a byword for all that was evil.

The imaginations of the Church Fathers, or at least their susceptibility to believing anti-Gnostic rumours started by others, reached a zenith in Epiphanius's account of a group he labelled the Borborites. The name derives from the Greek word *borboros*, meaning 'mud', so Borborite essentially meant one who was filthy, both physically and morally. Epiphanius claimed that the Borborites practised ritual homosexual intercourse and smeared themselves with menstrual blood and semen, which was then consumed as a form of eucharist. If that were not enough, they were also said to eat human foetuses. Such charges were part of the standard arsenal of accusations employed by the Church when seeking the moral high ground – similar accusations were later levelled against the Jews, witches, the Knights Templar[51] and even certain popes – and it would therefore be remarkably unlikely that the Borborites performed any of the things that were ascribed to them.

Sethians and Ophites

One thing we can assume about the Borborites is that they almost certainly would not have referred to themselves by that name and it is possible that the name is a corruption of Barbelo, Barbeloites or Barbelognostics. Barbelo is a name used in some forms of Gnosticism to denote the first emanation from the true God (known elsewhere as Ennoia, or Thought); it was regarded simultaneously as both feminine and androgynous. Confusingly, the Barbeloites may also not have referred to themselves by this name, as it was a term coined by the Church Fathers in their anti-Gnostic tirades; what name the Barbeloites did actually use has not been preserved, although they would have probably used a designation such as 'the holy' or 'the righteous', which were the names Gnostic groups commonly used to refer to themselves. The Barbeloites gave prominence to Barbelo in their texts, especially in the creation of the material world. Like the school of Marcus, they appear to have operated like a cult, with secret handshakes to make themselves known to other Barbeloites, although this may have merely been a practical necessity in the face of growing persecution from the Church.

The Barbeloites belong to a school of Gnosticism that scholars have labelled 'Sethian'; however, unlike the Barbeloites, the Sethians *do* seem to have referred to themselves by this name. The Sethians revered the figure of Seth, the third son of Adam and Eve after Cain and Abel. After seeing his two brothers fatally come to blows over the issue of offering sacrifices to the creator God, Seth was said to have gained *gnosis* after being instructed by Adam, who predicted that 'Seth and his seed', as the Nag Hammadi Apocalypse of Adam calls them, would continue to experience the liberating gift of *gnosis*, but would also experience persecution.

Persecution of typical Old Testament ferocity was soon experienced by the Sethians – and indeed all humanity – when the creator God sent the flood. This did not happen because the Demiurge wanted to punish mankind for its iniquity, as is the case in the traditional version of events, but because he was angry and jealous that Seth and his seed had acquired *gnosis*. The best way of making sure that no one else became a Gnostic initiate was quite simple: kill everyone. However, the Demiurge's subtle plan had not reckoned on a one-woman Gnostic resistance movement, in the person of Seth's sister, Norea. Norea was having trouble with her husband, a rather dim-witted Noah (at least that's how he's portrayed in the Gnostic texts, as we shall see in a later chapter). Noah had been instructed by the Demiurge to build an ark on the summit of Mount Seir, not Ararat as the traditional story in Genesis holds.[52] Suspecting a trap, Norea protests to her husband, but he won't listen. To make her point a little more forcefully, Norea burns the ark down, which so angers the Demiurge that he sends a legion of archons to rape Norea as punishment for her insubordination. Norea appeals for help to the true God, who hears her call and sends the aeon Eleleth (Sagacity) to save her and instruct her in the ways of Gnostic righteousness. The flood duly comes anyway, with Noah and his family being saved, not by taking refuge in the ark, but in a luminous cloud. Seth and Norea's respective descendants, the Gnostics, became known as 'the great race of Seth' and their texts, myths and stories form some of the most important Gnostic literature of all. We shall examine some of these in the later chapter.

Like the Sethians, the Ophites were a Gnostic school seemingly not founded by a teacher whose name has come down to us. In seeking the origin of Gnostic wisdom, they revered the Serpent in the Garden of Eden story as being the first revealer of *gnosis*. As with other versions of the Eden story, it is Eve who gains *gnosis* first and is therefore seen as superior to Adam. The Ophites seem to have been in existence by the end of the first century CE, mainly in Syria and Egypt and may have influenced – or included among their number – the Sethians. As with much Gnostic history, lack of primary sources leaves many groups and individuals rather vague. As Stephen Hoeller notes:

> The Gnostics... were more concerned with exiting from the terrible stream of history than they were of leaving a record of themselves. Those who are determined to overcome the world are not the people of history; theirs is more likely to be a kind of

shadow history or counterhistory, containing a few faint traces of their tenuous and reluctant presence.[53]

Seeing the Gnostics through the dark glass of history, therefore, is both inevitable and also not necessarily a bad thing. More important than the precise whys and wherefores of which group or teacher said or did a particular thing, is the existence of *gnosis* itself and the possibility of true liberation. This possibility has existed since the beginning of history, say the Gnostics, and continues to exist today. Indeed, it will always do so, regardless of whether the history books record it or not.

Organisation and Sacraments

Gnostic communities seem to have operated along similar lines, regardless of whether they were Valentinians, Cainites, Sethians or belonged to any other denomination of Gnosticism. Despite being charged with elitism by the Church Fathers, the Gnostics were surprisingly egalitarian in most other respects, drawing devotees from all levels of society. Perhaps the most defining feature of Gnostic groups was their disregard for authority and any sort of hierarchy. As we have noted, the Valentinians even went so far as to take it in turns to be minister during their services, including allowing women to offer the sacraments; this seems to have been typical of many other groups as well. Tertullian complains that 'one does not know who is a catechumen, who is a believer, they meet with one another (in the house of assembly), listen to one another and pray with one another'.[54]

Given the reverence for the divine feminine, usually personified as Sophia (and sometimes as Ennoia or Barbelo), it is not surprising that women played an active role in Gnosticism, often becoming teachers, missionaries or prophetesses in addition to the priestly roles they enjoyed. Aside from Alexandra, who taught in Alexandria alongside her husband Carpocrates, we also know the names of Marcellina, a disciple of Marcus, who taught in Rome in the middle of the second century, and Ptolemaeus's friend Flora, to whom he seems to have acted as spiritual adviser.

Another aspect of Gnosticism that irked the Church Fathers was what they saw as its disorganisation – until the discovery at Nag Hammadi, it was likewise assumed that Gnostics mainly occupied themselves with their own individual practices and myths. However, certain texts discovered at Nag Hammadi, like the Gospel of Philip, show that the Gnostics had sacraments that were, ironically, quite close to those of the mainstream Church. The Gospel of Philip lists five sacraments:[55] baptism, chrism, eucharist, redemption and the bridal chamber. 'The object of a Gnostic sacrament,' as Stephen Hoeller notes:

> ... is not merely temporary sanctification, as in the Roman Catholic doctrine of sacramental grace, but rather a total transformation, a change into the essence of the Godhead. The perfected Gnostic is not a follower of Christ, but a deified human being; he is another Christ.[56]

Baptism, as in the mainstream Church, enters the Gnostic into the faith. Given the importance that some Gnostics (such as the Italian Valentinians) placed on Jesus's own baptism at the hands of John the Baptist, its importance cannot be overstated. Becoming baptised was a way of showing that one had renounced one's former life and was entering a new one, which would lead ultimately to returning to the Pleroma and the true God. Chrism, like its counterpart in the mainstream Church, involves the use of holy oils, which were administered during what we would know as confirmation. Chrism committed the Gnostic to pursuing their path further, the oil linking them with the higher, true world of the Pleroma. Eucharist in the mainstream church is a thanksgiving for Christ's sacrifice, but in Gnosticism it is a thanksgiving for the liberating message of *gnosis* that

Christ brought into the world. Redemption, likewise, is not redemption from original sin, which does not exist in Gnosticism, but is redemption from ignorance. The greatest of the Gnostic sacraments, the bridal chamber, is also the least known, as it has no direct parallel in the Western Church. Mystics frequently portray the union between the soul and God as a divine marriage, and the bridal chamber might have been similarly regarded. It could be seen as a union between the Gnostic believer and the divine, or, in psychological terms, as the complete integration of the personality, of the reconciling of all the opposing forces within the human heart. It is also possible that the bridal chamber may have functioned as a deathbed rite, ensuring that the soon-to-be-departed fully escaped the clutches of the archons and the Demiurge, and reached the Pleroma.

In addition to sacraments, the Gnostics also used talismans and amulets in their practices. These were often inscribed with so-called 'barbarous words', which were not from any known language, being usually either long sequences of vowels that were to be chanted during rituals, or names of aeonic figures such as Abraxas. Abraxas, according to Gnostic myth, was a redeemed archon who rose above the Hebdomad to rule over it as an intercessionary figure between the Pleroma and the world of matter. Abraxas became a figure of veneration for many Gnostics and was often portrayed on gems and amulets as having the head of a rooster, the body of a man and serpents instead of legs. In one hand he held a whip, a shield in the other. This odd mixture of man and beast had symbolic meaning, with the rooster's head representing the dawn of understanding (roosters of course being the animal that traditionally greets the dawn) and a sense of vigilant wakefulness; the body of a man represents the embodied logos, the human capacity for understanding and growth; the snakes represent prudence and energy; while the whip and shield symbolise the dynamism of the life force and wisdom (the great protector) respectively.

Gnostic Religions

The Mandaeans

At the same time as the various groups discussed in the previous chapter were active, all or most of whom we could regard as 'Christian Gnostics' (although the early Sethians could have been Jewish), a fully fledged Gnostic religion appeared in what is now Iraq. The Mandaean faith differs from most of the beliefs of the Gnostics we have examined in the previous chapter in that it was primarily non-Christian and was also an organised religion. And, again unlike the Gnostics so far mentioned, the Mandaeans still exist to this day. This is perhaps attributable to the fact that Muslims regarded them as one of the Peoples of the Book, which protected them from persecution, while European missionaries mistook them for Christians, describing them as 'John Christians', a reference to the Mandaean reverence for John the Baptist. Their survival is also due, in part, to the almost impenetrable cloak of secrecy that has separated them from other Iraqi peoples.

Their origins are obscure – they may have originally been a breakaway Jewish group, but this is still conjectural – and we are not even sure what the word Mandaean actually means. One theory holds that it derives from the Aramaic word *manda*, meaning 'knowledge'. Another theory suggests that the name derives from *mandi,* which refers to the fenced-off enclosure in which Mandaean rituals are performed, in which the sole building is the Mandaean equivalent of a temple, called the *bit manda*, meaning 'house of knowledge'; in this etymology, Mandaean therefore means 'one who uses the house of knowledge'. A third theory holds that the name is a reference to the mythical redeemer Manda d-Hiia, who was said to have been in Jerusalem at the same time as Jesus and whose name means 'knowledge of life'.[57]

Gnosis, as we have already noted, also means 'knowledge', and it is usually assumed that Mandaean therefore also means 'gnostic'. However, Edmondo Lupieri suggests that this is not quite the case, as the Mandaeans distinguish between two classes among themselves, the *nasuraiia* and the *mandaiia*. The *nasuraiia* are 'those who possess *nasurita,* which is knowledge of the gnostic kind, while the *mandaiia* refers to ordinary believers. All priests are expected to be *nasuraiia*, but all *nasuraiia* are not necessarily priests.[58]

The Mandaeans revere John the Baptist, but regard Moses, Abraham and Jesus – and, later on, the Prophet Muhammad – as false teachers. Given this, it is perhaps not surprising that they attach great significance to the sacrament of baptism, insisting it must be done in fresh running water, which they believe originally comes from the realm of the true God. All Mandaean chapels are therefore built by rivers or streams, with baptisms usually being carried out in the spring or summer.

Burial is the next most important Mandaean ritual. The deceased would be interred in an unmarked grave, the absence of a headstone symbolising the lack of importance of the earthly body compared to the divine spark within each person. Ceremonies would then be held for periods of up to 40 days to ensure that the departed successfully escaped the material world and returned home to the world of light.

Mandaean cosmology has the two Gods of Gnosticism, the true God and the creator God, who inhabit the worlds of light and darkness respectively. The material world, as in Christian Gnosticism, comes into being after a series of emanations, with the creator God being known as Ptahil. Human beings were created by

Ptahil, except for their souls, which came from the world of light. It is these souls or sparks of light within each person that Mandaeanism seeks to liberate. Unlike Christian Gnosticism, it is not *gnosis* alone that liberates, but also observance of the Mandaean sacraments of baptism, liturgy and burial.

Mandaean Texts

The principal Mandaean text is the Ginza, meaning 'treasure', also known as the 'Great Book'. It is divided into two sections, the Right Ginza, which contains mythological and theological texts, and the Left Ginza, which is made up of songs and burial rituals. As with much Gnostic material, Mandaean liturgies and sacred writings are strikingly powerful as poetry. The cosmology described in the Ginza makes use of water as a metaphor for the world of light:

> The great Jordan came alive,
> And the living water was in it.
> Luminous water came alive from the living water.
> I, life, came alive
> And all the uthras – the light beings – found space.[59]

When Ptahil, the Demiurge, creates life, water symbolism is again employed:

> He [Ptahil's father] dressed me in a radiant robe and wrapped me
> in a covering of light.
> He gave me a major crown in whose luminosity
> the worlds glisten
> And he said to me, 'Son, go to the Tibil [physical] earth
> and make the black waters solid.
> Solidify the Tibil earth and inscribe Jordan rivers
> and canals upon its face.[60]

Water again features in the contrasting depictions of Jesus and John the Baptist. Jesus is described as a sorcerer who 'perverts the living baptism and baptises them in blocked waters'.[61] John, on the other hand, baptises 'in the white Jordan of living and brilliant waters, clothe him in garments of radiance, and cover him in turbans of light'.[62] The Ginza has harsher words for Jesus:

> After John, the world will go on in lies and Christ the Roman will split the peoples; the twelve seducers [the disciples] wander the world. [...] the light being Anosh [a redeemer figure] comes. He will expose the lies of Jesus the liar, who makes himself equal to the angels of light. He will accuse Christ the Roman, the liar, the son of a woman, who did not come from the world of light.[63]

The Ginza, while being the central Mandaean text, is not their only scripture. Perhaps the next most important is the Book of John, which contains stories of John the Baptist's life and teachings. John's birth is prophesied, with the result that the priests of the Jerusalem Temple attempted to have him murdered while still an infant. The adult John is presented as the ideal Mandaean, wise to the lies of both the Jerusalem clergy and his great rival, Jesus the sorcerer.

The Manichaeans

Manichaeism was founded by the Persian prophet Mani (215–277), who was brought up in Babylon as an Elchasaite, a Jewish Christian sect who were also known as *katharoi* (the pure ones). After a series of divine revelations, Mani attempted to reform the Elchasaites, but was denounced and thrown out. Undeterred, he began a vigorous missionary campaign with three former Elchasaites (one of whom being his father) to proselytise what Mani called the Religion of Light. Mani claimed that he was of the same tradition as Seth,

Zoroaster, the Buddha and Jesus, but that these earlier masters had not revealed the whole truth, the revelation of which was his mission and his alone. Mani's doctrine was formulated to appeal to as many people as possible, taking ideas from Zoroastrianism, Christianity and Buddhism, whose aim was to unite and save humanity in one overarching faith. Seeking inspiration from a variety of traditions is something of a Gnostic trait, but there are also other aspects of Manichaeism that are Gnostic.

Like Bardaisan before him, Mani experienced court patronage for many years under the Persian Kings Shapur (241–72) and his son Hormizd (272–3). When Hormizd's brother Bahram came to the throne in 273, Mani fell from favour, having made enemies amongst the Zoroastrian priesthood, who were eager to see this self-styled prophet be put in his place. Mani was subject to a kangaroo court, sentenced to death and thrown into prison. He experienced 26 days of agony wearing heavy chains, which Manichaeans referred to as Mani's Passion, before expiring. His body was decapitated and his head was displayed above one of the city gates.

Mani's cosmology was radically dualist, in that it posits eternally pre-existent kingdoms of light and darkness. The darkness, ever agitated and jealous of the light, decides to attack it and, in its defence, the light sends the Primal Man (not to be confused with Adam) and his five sons to do battle with the darkness. The Primal Man's offspring are the aeons of the light breeze, wind, light, water and fire, and in battle they face the archons of smoke, fire, darkness, scorching wind and fog. The archons win the day, with the result that the Primal Man and his aeonic offspring are subsumed into the darkness. The God of Light now rescues the Primal Man, but in the course of the operation, the soul is left behind in the Darkness.

This leads to a new task: that of separating the soul or light particles out from the Darkness in which it remains trapped; to this end, a figure known as the Messenger emanates from the God of

Light. The Messenger has a cunning plan to retrieve the light: he sends out 12 beautiful Angels of Light to arouse the archons. The archons emit both sin and light at the sight of the angels; the sin descends downwards into the world of matter, where it becomes trapped in animals and plant life. Meanwhile, the Messenger and the angels begin to collect the light particles for transportation back to the world of light. Seeing this, the King of Darkness gathers up what light particles he can and creates two beings in which to trap the light: Adam and Eve.

To assist the Messenger in the work of collecting the remaining sparks of divine light from Adam and Eve, the 'Luminous' Jesus is sent into the world in order to awaken them. However, unlike in most other Gnostic versions of Eden, here it is Adam who is the first to eat of the Tree of Knowledge, and at Jesus's prompting at that, while Eve – having been instructed in the pleasures of the flesh by the archons of the Dark Lord – has other things on her mind. This leads to the births of the first children, Cain and Abel, and from then on, the Messenger can't stop the reproductive process of humans, the subsequent proliferation of humanity making it ever harder for all the light to be gathered back together. As a sort of divine 'Plan B', the Messenger then instructs Jesus that he must extend his saving mission to all of humanity, across all time.

It should be noted that the Manichaean conception of Jesus was that of the 'Luminous' or 'Heavenly' Jesus who appears in other Gnostic texts, who is not the same as the Biblical 'Jesus of Nazareth'.[64] The Manichaean Jesus did indeed descend into the physical first-century Jesus, who was seen as human, not divine, and to whom the Manichaeans ascribe no particular teachings (they did not accept the New Testament or its gospels). Furthermore, the 'real' Jesus (the Luminous one) did not suffer on the Cross, but only appeared to do so (the human Jesus who housed his spirit suffered), a belief which ties Manichaeism to the Docetic heresy frequently adopted by the Gnostics. The Luminous Jesus was also thought to have descended into other great teachers throughout history, including Seth, Zarathustra, the Buddha and also Mani himself, and was also thought to be present throughout nature as part of his ongoing struggle to free the light from matter. As a consequence of this belief, Mani often told his followers to be careful not to walk on insects that crossed their path, nor to accidentally tread on plants, all of which were thought to have light particles trapped within them.

It would be impractical, of course, to expect everyone to observe such strictures and so two distinct classes of Manichaean emerged, the Elect and the Listeners. The Elect were the faith's priesthood, practising strict asceticism by abstaining from meat, wine, blasphemy and sex. The Listeners – the ordinary believers of Mani's church – were also expected to observe certain rules, such as regular confession to the priests, to whom they also gave money for their upkeep. Listeners were allowed to own property and marry but were forbidden to have children. Manichaeism, like radically dualist Christian Gnosticism, had a hostility towards all things to do with the body, which it regarded as nothing more than a vessel that had the light imprisoned within it.

Manichaean Texts

So effective was the Church's campaigns against Manichaeism, that it led to the destruction of nearly all their sacred literature. (The anti-Manichaean drives in ninth-century China were likewise almost equally effective in this respect.) Thought lost forever, a number of texts were discovered at ruined Manichaean monasteries in China between 1904 and 1914; this was effectively a 'Manichaean Nag Hammadi'. Discoveries were also made in Egypt in 1929, with further texts coming to light in 1969. These recoveries revolutionised our understanding of Manichaeism and allowed Mani and his followers to speak with their own voices for the first time in over a millennium.

The Kephalaia is a collection of teachings that covers most of the central tenets of the faith, usually taking the form of a student (sometimes opponent) asking Mani a question, to which he gives answers of varying lengths:

The student asks: [...] What is the light mind?

The messenger [Mani] responds:

If I tell you these things you care about
and they become true after your concern,
will you understand what you must do?
I will give vision to those who see!
I will make the living fountain overflow
so the thirsty may drink and live.[65]

The figure of Jesus recurs in Manichaean scriptures, in a somewhat more favourable light than in Mandaean texts:

This name Jesus, there is a grace surrounding it. For it is Jesus who gives repentance to the penitent.

He stands in our midst... he is not far from us, my brothers, even as he said in his preaching: 'I am as close to you as the raiment of your body!' [66]

As with the Mandaean texts, there is some striking imagery to convey the impact of *gnosis*:

Let us bless our Lord Jesus who has sent to us the Spirit of Truth! He came and separated us from the error of the world, he brought

us a mirror in which he looked and saw the universe.[67]
Jesus dug a river in the cosmos. He dug a river,
even he of the sweet name. He dug it with a spade
of truth. He dredged it with a basket of wisdom...[68]

Of the other Manichaean scriptures that have been recovered,
we can identify the Book of Giants, which is actually a Manichaean
version of part of the apocryphal Book of Enoch; various texts
dealing with Mani's life and passion; and numerous texts dealing
with Manichaean cosmology and cosmogony.

Hermeticism

Of the other main non-Christian forms of Gnosticism, Hermeticism
is the most important. Its origins are obscure, being traditionally
described as coming from the great sage Hermes Trismegistus. In
reality, the writings said to have been written by Hermes, known as
the Corpus Hermeticum, were probably composed in the early centuries of our era, most likely in Alexandria. Hermeticism shares with
Gnosticism a belief in two Gods, the creator and the transcendent,
real God. There is no redeemer figure, however, and the Hermetic
initiate can only be saved through his or her own effort and by
attaining the salvific *gnosis*. Although nature is seen as fallen, it has the
potential to become restored to a divine state through the interven-
tion of the Hermeticists, who regarded themselves as the stewards of
nature. Indeed, the divine is present in nature and careful work with
natural substances – alchemy – was thought to bring out the divinity
in both nature and the adept. Rather like the Valentinians, the
Hermeticists regarded each person who gained *gnosis* as helping not
just themselves but the whole of material creation.

The Nag Hammadi library contains several hermetic works: the
Prayer of Thanksgiving, Asclepius and the Discourse on the Eighth
and Ninth. Of these, the latter two are significant. Asclepius is a

dialogue between Hermes Trismegistus and his student, Asclepius, which covers topics from Tantric sex to idol worship to the nature of the soul. It is with regard to the soul that the text has most to say, stressing the importance of man's potential for spiritual evolution and *gnosis*:

> 'The gods know the things of men know the things of gods. And I am speaking about men, Asclepius, who have attained learning and knowledge. But about those who are more vain than these, it is not fitting that we say anything base, since we are divine and are introducing holy matters.'[69]

Hermes informs Asclepius that the spiritual path is an arduous one, which could also bring derision and mockery on the seeker, as the world is seemingly overrun with the impious and the vain:

> 'Darkness will be preferred to light and death will be preferred to life. No one will gaze into heaven. And the pious man will be counted as insane, and the impious man will be honoured as wise. The man who is afraid will be considered as strong. And the good man will be punished like a criminal.'[70]

The Discourse on the Eighth and Ninth also takes the form of a dialogue (as does much of the Corpus Hermeticum), this time concerning the ascent of the soul through the upper spheres of the cosmos. The eighth sphere was seen as the upper limit of the Ogdoad, so any progress towards the ninth was a sign that the soul was almost free of the influence of the archons. In the text, Hermes Trismegistus informs his unnamed and incredulous student that the power to make this ascent is within us:

> 'Indeed the understanding dwells in you; in me it is as though the power were pregnant. For when I conceived from the fountain that flowed to me, I gave birth.'

'My father, you have spoken every word well to me. But I am amazed at this statement that you have just made. For you said "The power that is in me."'[71]

Hermes teaches his student to be vigilant with his prayers, as the attainment of spiritual maturity is a divine gift:

'I am singing a hymn within myself. While you rest yourself, be active in praise. For you have found what you seek.'
'But it is proper, my father, that I praise because I am filled in my heart?'
'What is proper is your praise that you will sing to God so that it might be written in this imperishable book.'[72]

Some of the prayers and invocations that Hermes and his student utter contain chants and so-called 'barbarous words' – words from no known language which were used in Gnostic rituals. They were probably intoned or even sung:

'I have received life from you, when you made me wise. I praise you. I call your name that is hidden within me: a o ee o eee ooo iii oooo ooooo ooooo uuuuuu oo ooooooooo ooooooooo oo. You are the one who exists with the spirit. I sing a hymn to you reverently.'[73]

Another important Hermetic text is Poimandres, which elucidates a dualistic view of the mind and body; the former is related to light, truth, the eternal and ultimate salvation, while the latter is depicted as being dark, deceptive, temporal and mortal. In Poimandres, the world is acknowledged as being imperfect but, although created by the Demiurge, he is not held to blame for the state of things. Human beings are depicted as descending into this world, a world they must ultimately transcend if they are to return to the divine source. Upon reaching the eighth sphere, the soul is regarded as achieving divinity:

They surrender to the [aeonic] powers, and become the powers, and are in god. This is the good, the aim of those who have gnosis: to become god.[74]

The concept of 'becoming god' has an echo in the Gospel of Philip, where the Gnostic is described as 'no longer a Christian, but Christ'. In the thirteenth book of the Corpus Hermeticum, Hermes Trismegistus explains *gnosis* to his son Tat:

Hermes: Even so it is my son, when a man is born again; it is no longer a body of three dimensions that he perceives but the incorporeal.

Tat: Father, now that I see in mind, I see myself to be the All. I am in heaven and in earth, in water and in air; I am in beasts and plants; I am a babe in the womb, and one that is not yet conceived, and one who has been born; I am present everywhere.

Hermes: Now, my son, you know what the rebirth is.[75]

Jewish Gnosticism

Certain Gnostic groups, such as the Sethians, may have originally been Jewish, formed as a response to the changes within both Judaism and Palestine at the time. The Nag Hammadi library certainly contains texts that have significant Jewish elements, such as *On the Origin of the World* and the *Hypostasis of the Archons*, and these texts are probably the heritage of the Judaic matrix out of which Gnosticism grew. With the rise of classical Gnosticism, which we can broadly categorise as Christian, Jewish Gnostic groups seemed to disappear altogether. The most likely explanation is that they developed into Christian groups, just as Christianity itself started out as a breakaway branch of Judaism.

Given the uncertainty over the fate of Jewish Gnostic groups in the early centuries of the Common Era, it is therefore a matter of continued debate amongst scholars as to the extent of Gnostic tendencies within the Jewish tradition after that date. Some, such as the prominent Jewish scholar Gershom Scholem, have argued that the most Gnostic element within Judaism was Kabbalism, which emerged in the twelfth century in the writings of scholars such as Isaac the Blind, and the Book of the Bahir in particular, which he is thought to have written. Others have countered this, arguing that Kabbalism came from an exclusively Jewish milieu; such arguments recall the debate as to whether Gnosticism was a Christian heresy, or a completely separate, syncretistic faith.[76] Nevertheless, it is worth briefly noting some similarities between Gnostic and Kabbalistic thought. Kabbala, which means 'receiving', shares with Gnosticism a God beyond all description; God cannot be described, only experienced. Furthermore, God has a female companion, Shekinah, recalling the Gnostic Ennoia. The material world is seen as imperfect, but this state of affairs can be positively influenced by the Kabbalist, who can effect a healing. (The same idea can be found in Hermeticism.) Like Gnosticism, Kabbalistic knowledge is esoteric, only available to the initiate. Codes and ciphers play a prominent part, recalling the Gnostic gems inscribed with barbarous words. In both cases, the uninitiated would only see gibberish; only the Kabbalist and Gnostic would understand the true meaning of the text. This magical side of Kabbalism caused its practitioners to be regarded as virtual heretics in some communities, the more orthodox concerned that fear of the Kabbalists would cause an increase in anti-Semitism. Gnostics, likewise, were notorious for their heresy, at least in the eyes of the Church Fathers.

Islamic Gnosticism

Charges of heresy also befell Gnostic elements within Islam. These were the Shi'ite *ghulats*, meaning 'exaggerators' or 'extremists', whose most notable early figure was Abdullah ibn Saba, 'a figure comparable to Simon Magus in the history of Christian Gnosticism'.77 Other groups followed in ibn Saba's wake: the Assassins, the Druze, the Sufis, to name but three, all of whom could be said to have Gnostic aspects. The Sufis were certainly no strangers to charges of heresy: the great Sufi teacher Mansur al Hallaj (*c.* 858–922) proclaimed 'I am the Truth' and was crucified as a heretic and blasphemer. Despite appearances to the contrary, he was not trying to put himself above God. Rather, his statement was an admission that there was, after years of meditation, prayer and communion, no al-Hallaj left: there was only God within the body of al-Hallaj. Such an extreme form of mystic realisation is nothing other than gnosis.

Indeed, there is a close correlation between mysticism and Gnosticism: both stress the importance of the *experience* and the unimportance of dogma. The difference lies mainly in that mystics tend to posit the existence of one god, while the Gnostics acknowledge two. There is certainly an awareness of two worlds in Sufism, as the thirteenth-century master Abd' al-Khâliq Ghijduwâni states:

Your journey is towards your homeland. Remember you are travelling from the world of appearances to the world of Reality.78

It is thought that Gnostic ideas reached the Arab world via foreign converts to Islam, especially during the early years of Islamic expansion in the seventh and eighth centuries CE. 'This may help to explain how certain stories about Jesus came to appear in Islam, stories that do not have any equivalent in the canonical Christian gospels. They are, however, very close in spirit to the Gnostic gospels, such as the Gospel of Thomas. The Sufi mystic and theologian Abu Hamid Muhammad al-Ghazali (1058–1111) recorded a number of these sayings in his book *The Revival of the Religious Sciences*:

> Jesus said, 'Whoever knows and does and teaches will be called great in the kingdom of heaven.'

> Jesus said, 'Evil scholars are like a rock that has fallen at the mouth of a brook: it does not drink the water, nor does it let the water flow to the plants. And evil scholars are like the drainpipe of a latrine that is plastered outside but filthy inside; or like graves that are decorated outside but contain dead people's bones inside.'

> Jesus was asked, 'Who taught you?'
> He answered, 'No one taught me. I saw that the ignorance of the fool was shameful, so I avoided it.'

> One day Jesus was walking with his students, and they passed by the carcass of a dog.
> The students said, 'How this dog stinks!'
> But Jesus said, 'How white are its teeth!'[79]

> Jesus said, 'Whoever seeks the world is like one who drinks seawater. The more he drinks, the more his thirst increases, until it kills him.'[80]

Gnostic ideas find their way into the Mother of Books, one of the key texts of Islamic Gnosticism, written in the late eighth century. It takes the form of a dialogue between Jabir and his master Baqir covering cosmology and cosmogony. The arrogant world ruler is Azazi'il, whose name perhaps derived from the Jewish fallen angel, Azazel. In contrast, the true God is unknown, portrayed as a king behind a curtain. It is only through knowledge and prayer that he can become known:

The one who knows arises
and testifies to spirit as to himself.[81]

The Yezidis

The Sufis may also have been partially responsible for the creation
of an entirely separate, non-Muslim faith that has distinctly Gnostic
aspects. The Yezidis, a mainly Kurdish-speaking semi-nomadic
people who live in what is now northern Iraq, Syria, Armenia and
Turkey, seem to have emerged in the twelfth century CE from the
followers of the Sufi master Sheik 'Adı- ibn Musa-fir (c. 1073/78–
1162). When European explorers first encountered it in the 1830s,
the Yezidi faith was thought to be 'a kind of Manichaeism'.[82] They
were also thought to worship the devil, giving the Yezidis the kind
of notoriety achieved by such Gnostic groups as the Cainites and the
Borborites.

While Sheikh 'Adī, who is held in high regard by many Yezidis,
would no doubt not have approved of such rumours, we can note
some shared ground with the Gnostics, Cainites, Borborites, or
otherwise: like Gnosticism, its origins are unclear – as well as
Sufism, it could be descended from Zoroastrianism or one of the
other Iranian mystery schools; like Manichaeism, it is syncretistic; it
also has links with Alevism (who are regarded as *ghulats* by orthodox
Muslims, which would tend to support a gnostic basis to Yezidism)
and Yârsânism. As with the Gnostic schools, the Yezidis have no
trouble with myth (including myths of their own beginnings), and
they also have no centralised form of the faith –Yezidi worship tends
to vary from area to area, with their respective sheikhs teaching
their followers different prayers. And again, like Gnosticism, the
Yezidis hold that anyone can become divine: their priests are seen as
representing important figures such as Melek Tawus or Sheik 'Adī,
and are literally, therefore, the same as God.

Although the Yezidis have an oral culture, they have sacred writings such as the *Jilwe* (the Splendour or Unveiling) and *Meshef Resh* (the Black Book), which were discovered by Westerners in the early twentieth century. Their creation myths have a Gnostic flavour. In the beginning, God creates a white pearl from his own essence that contains all the elements that are to form the universe. He then – some versions say 40,000 years later – creates a Heptad of angels to rule over the world and makes Melek Tawus the chief amongst them. God then creates the seven heavens, the earth, the sun and the moon, and it is left to Melek Tawus to create human beings and all the animals. Each member of the Heptad has dominion over one of the four elements or the plant, animal and human realms; all the elements must be respected and not polluted in any way.

Melek Tawus is revered by the Yezidis as the greatest of the angels and is known as the 'Lord of this World' and also as the 'Peacock Angel', and all earthly affairs are said to be under his influence. In Christianity, 'the Lord of this World' is none other than Lucifer, who is regarded as a fallen angel, as he is in Islam also. The inability – or reluctance – of both Christians and Muslims to understand Yezidism has led to the mistaken assumption that the Yezidis are devil worshippers. To this day, they remain persecuted by secular authorities and also by Muslims, who do not regard them as 'People of the Book'.

Texts and Gospels

The Nag Hammadi discovery is the single largest and best known find of Gnostic documents in history. The texts, as we have noted, were bound into 13 leather codices and their contents offer us direct access into the mystic, mythic world of Gnosticism. Of the 52 works that comprise the Nag Hammadi library, 40 were previously unknown. The texts fall into a number of loose categories, such as creation myths, liturgical and ritual texts, writings on various Gnostic themes such as the nature of the soul and the Divine Feminine, the sayings of Jesus, the lives of the Apostles, as well as a small number of Hermetic texts and a section of Plato's *Republic*. There were originally further works that have not survived, or are so fragmentary that nothing can be gleaned from them. While it is beyond the scope of our present discussion to study the entire Nag Hammadi library, a few of the more important texts are the ones that follow.

The Apocryphon of John

The Apocryphon, or Secret Book, of John, contains one of the most detailed Gnostic creation myths that has come down to us. Thought to have been based on an earlier Jewish text, the Apocryphon of John was Christianised to feature the figure of Jesus, who appears throughout as the Revealer, and recounts the mysteries of creation to the apostle John, the narrator. The Secret Book was widely copied and belongs to the Sethian school of Gnosticism; it has been suggested that they even regarded it as the sequel to the Gospel of John. Its main theme is the origin of evil, and how we can escape it and return to the Pleroma.

The text opens with John at the Temple in Jerusalem, some time after the Crucifixion. A Pharisee appears and mocks him, telling him that his teacher (Jesus) has filled his head with lies, 'closed your minds, and turned you from the traditions of your parents'.[83] Troubled, John flees to a mountain to contemplate, when suddenly the heavens open and Jesus appears to him in the form of a child, then as an old man and finally as a youth. He consoles John, telling him 'I am with you always. I am the father, I am the mother, I am the child. I am the incorruptible and the undefiled one.'[84]

Jesus begins to recount the story of creation, beginning with a description of the true God, describing him as 'pure light into which no eye can gaze'.

> The One is illimitable, since there is nothing before it to limit it,
> Unfathomable, since there is nothing before it to fathom it,
> Immeasurable, since there was nothing before to measure it,
> Invisible, since nothing has seen it,
> Eternal, since it exists eternally,
> Unutterable, since there is nothing before it to give it a name.
> [...]
> The One is a realm that gives a realm, life that gives life, a blessed one that gives blessedness, knowledge that gives knowledge, a good one that gives goodness, mercy that gives mercy and redemption, grace that gives grace.[85]

The true God, enamoured with his own reflection, emanates Barbelo and her attributes are listed: 'her light shines like the father's light; she, the perfect power, is the image of the perfect and invisible virgin spirit... the perfect glory among the realms, the glory of revelation'.[86] The Christ child is then born to Barbelo, followed by the emanation of the aeons and the appearance of the first human, Geradamas. His name probably means 'Adam the stranger', implying that Adam is a stranger to the created world of matter, whose real home is the eternal realm of light. The fall occurs when Sophia desires to bring forth a being without the approval or knowledge of her consort. The being she produces is Ialdabaoth, who 'did not resemble its mother and was misshapen' and has 'the figure of a snake with the face of a lion. Its eyes were like flashing bolts of lightning'.[87]

Ialdabaoth, believing himself to be the only god, takes power from his mother and produces from his own mindlessness the first archons, who rule over each sphere of the heavens. It is clear that the Demiurge's creation is flawed:

> When the light mixed with darkness, it made the darkness shine. When darkness mixed with light, it dimmed the light and became neither light nor darkness, but rather gloom.[88]

Sophia, feeling depleted after Ialdabaoth's theft of some of her light, repents 'with many tears'. The beings in the Pleroma hear her and offer her praises to the great virgin spirit, who accepts Sophia's repentance. Sophia must remain in the ninth sphere 'until she restored what was lacking in herself'.[89]

A voice calls out in Ialdabaoth's realm, 'The man exists and the son of Man', which the Demiurge thinks is his mother calling him. He doesn't realise that this is the true God speaking to him, who then appears to the arrogant creator God in human form.

Inspired by this divine encounter, Ialdabaoth and a team of archons create Adam's soul. A still greater array of archons then create his body, each of them being given a specific job, from Raphao, who creates Adam's head, down to Miamai, who does the toenails. A further detachment of archons is required to animate

Adam, again with each one being given responsibility for a particular body part, but try as they might they can't bring Adam to life.

A group of aeons descend in order to recover Sophia's light and advise Ialdabaoth to breathe life into Adam himself. Ialdabaoth does so, unaware that he has breathed light into Adam. Having some of Sophia's power within him, Adam immediately comes to life. Ialdabaoth and the archons become jealous, recognising that Adam has superior intelligence to any of them. They throw Adam into 'the lowest part of the whole material realm'.

Eve joins Adam in the Garden of Eden; Jesus, in the form of an eagle, bids them to eat the fruit of the tree of life. Ialdabaoth becomes jealous that Eve has attained *gnosis* and rapes her. This results in the birth of Cain and Abel. It is only with her third child, Seth, that Eve has a child with Adam.

Christ then speaks to John about human destiny, the fate of believers (Gnostics) and those who 'had knowledge but turned away'.[90] The Apocryphon ends with Jesus's hymn, in which he declares himself to be 'the light dwelling in light' and 'let whoever hears arise from deep sleep'.[91]

Other Nag Hammadi texts offer variant versions of Gnostic cosmology and cosmogony, among them the Hypostasis of the Archons, On the Origin of the World, the Apocalypse of Adam and the Paraphrase of Shem; lack of space in the present volume sadly prevents discussion here.

The Gospel of Truth

The Gospel of Truth is a Valentinian gospel, thought by some to be the work of Valentinus himself. The gospel is mentioned by Irenaeus, which dates it to around the middle of the second century, which would make Valentinus's authorship all the more plausible. It is generally considered to be one of the gems of the entire Nag Hammadi collection. Unlike the canonical gospels, which all recount Jesus's life and ministry as a narrative, the Gospel of Truth is typical of Gnostic gospels in that narrative is largely absent. The gospel is essentially a poetic exegesis, portraying Jesus as a 'quiet guide' who has come to reveal the mysteries of the hidden father, ignorance of whom can only lead to terror and fear. Jesus confounds the other scribes and teachers, claiming that they were foolish since they tried to understand the world by analysing the law. It is only knowledge which leads to salvation, not adhering to the letter of the law. Jesus's crucifixion is seen as the price to be paid for bringing the good news of *gnosis* to 'the empty territory of fears'.

In a celebrated passage, ignorance is likened to a nightmare:

Either they are fleeing somewhere, or they lack strength to escape when pursued. They are involved in inflicting blows, or they themselves receive bruises. They are falling from high places, or they fly through the air with no wings at all. Other times, it is as if certain people were trying to kill them, even though there is no one pursuing them; or they themselves are killing those beside them, and they are stained by their blood. Until the moment when they who are passing through all these things – I mean they who have experienced all these confusions – awaken, they see nothing because the dreams were nothing.[92]

Awakening, the gaining of *gnosis*, the gospel states, is the only way out of the nightmare of material existence.

The Gospel of Thomas

Arguably the most famous Nag Hammadi text, the Gospel of Thomas was in fact partially discovered at Oxyrhynchus when three Greek fragments were unearthed in 1897, with further fragments coming to light six years later. However, it wasn't until the complete text was recovered at Nag Hammadi (like the rest of the library, a Coptic translation), that scholars realised what they had had in their possession all that time.[93]

The Gospel of Thomas is important in a number of ways. Although the Nag Hammadi Coptic version dates from the fourth century CE, the original Greek Thomas may have dated from as early as the first half of the second century. The gospel has been dated to around 140 by Gilles Quispel, but it has also been suggested that this was merely the date of the writing down of much earlier sayings. Indeed, the Gospel of Thomas, in its earliest, oral form, could date from 50–100 CE, making it contemporaneous with the four canonical gospels, if not earlier. If it is indeed this early, as evidence and scholarly opinion now suggest, then the Gospel of Thomas moves well beyond 'heresy'; indeed, it has been speculated that it may include original sayings of Jesus that were not recorded by the authors of the four canonical gospels. This in itself gives Gnosticism a major claim (if one were needed) to being a valid spiritual – and Christian – tradition dating back to the time of the Apostles. This is precisely the same lineage that the Roman Catholic Church uses to claim that *it* is the one true Church; the Gospel of Thomas, a stark, beautiful, poetic document of wisdom, would suggest otherwise.

Thomas differs from the canonicals in that it is not a narrative gospel of Jesus's ministry and passion. As we have already seen, it presents itself as 'the secret words which the living Jesus spoke and Didymus Judas Thomas wrote down'.[94] Judas Thomas is Jesus's twin brother according to Syrian tradition, although whether 'twin' actually meant sibling in the sense of being related by blood, or was instead a metaphor for Thomas's spiritual development, is unclear.[95] In declaring itself 'secret', the Gospel of Thomas is nailing its Gnostic colours to the mast: these, it is saying, are the *true* teachings of Jesus, intended for 'those who have ears to hear'. It is made up of 114 sayings attributed to Jesus which, in the Nag Hammadi original, are unnumbered; the numbers were later added by scholars for the sake of clarity.

The Gospel of Thomas does not appear to have a structure: the sayings are of various kinds, from proverbs and parables to ethics and eschatology. Jesus is portrayed not as the worker of miracles, healer of the sick or the raiser of the dead, but as a spiritual teacher:

> Let him who seeks continue seeking until he finds. When he finds, he will become troubled. When he becomes troubled, he will be astonished, and he will rule over all.[96]

The emphasis both here and elsewhere in the Gospel of Thomas is on the personal nature of spiritual life: it is the disciple who has to walk the spiritual path, not Jesus. Saying 70 emphasises this:

> Jesus said, 'If you bring forth what is within you, what you have will save you. If you do not have that within you, what you do not have within you [will] kill you.'[97]

It is not Christ's death on the cross – of which no mention is made in Thomas – that will save, but regular spiritual practice and observing certain basic precepts, such as those outlined in Saying 6:

> His disciples questioned him and said to him, 'Do you want us to fast? How shall we pray? Shall we give alms? What diet shall we observe?'
>
> Jesus said, 'Do not tell lies, and do not do what you hate, for all things are plain in the sight of heaven. For nothing hidden will not become manifest, and nothing covered will remain without being uncovered.'[98]

Despite Jesus appearing to be something of a Zen Buddhist in the Gospel of Thomas, there are numerous parallels with the four canonical gospels.[99] For instance, Saying 5 proclaims that 'there is nothing hidden that will not be revealed'. This is echoed in Mark 4:22, 'Whatever is hidden away will be brought out into the open, and whatever is covered up will be uncovered.' Saying 33, 'What you will hear in your ear, in the other ear proclaim from your rooftops. After all, no one lights a lamp and puts it under a basket, nor does one put it in a hidden place. Rather, one puts it on a lampstand so that all who come and go will see its light', parallels similar pronouncements in the Synoptic gospels.[100] The parable of the lost sheep in Saying 107 reappears in modified form in Matthew (18:12–14) and Luke (15:4–7).

Despite these, and other, parallels with the canonical gospels,[101] Thomas has an ascetic, Gnostic quality that is all its own. Jesus advises his followers to 'be passers by' (Saying 42)[102] and not get embroiled in the world of those who do not have the ears to hear the word of *gnosis*, and who busy themselves by proclaiming their own apparent righteousness: 'He said, Lord there are many around the drinking trough, but there is nothing in the well' (Saying 74). These people, the narrow-minded, the dogmatically religious, the hylics, do not see reality as it actually is, as Saying 113 suggests:

His disciples said to him 'When will the kingdom come?'
He said, 'It will not come by waiting for it. It will not be a matter of saying "here it is" or "there it is". Rather, the kingdom of the father is spread out upon the earth, and men do not see it.'

The Treatise on the Resurrection

The concept of people being unable to see or hear the truth recurs throughout Gnostic literature; likewise the idea of people even being unable to read the scriptures properly and understand what they really mean. Gnostics would feel able to do so themselves, which accounts for the Gnostic tendency to interpret both their own and canonical scriptures in ways guaranteed to annoy the likes of Irenaeus. The Gnostics viewed St Paul, for instance, as one of their own when he described his conversion to Christ on the road to Damascus. Paul writes that he 'was snatched up into the highest heaven', but was unable to tell 'whether this actually happened or whether it was a vision'. During this experience, Paul 'heard things which cannot be put into words, things that human lips may not speak'.[103]

The Gnostic view of the resurrection, as we might expect, differs markedly from the orthodox position. The Nicene Creed states that Jesus 'suffered and was buried, and the third day he rose again'. This resurrection is bodily, which will one day be experienced by all, as the Creed states 'we look for the resurrection of the dead'. The Gnostic text known as the Treatise on the Resurrection, however, regards the Resurrection as something that is not physical at all, something 'which is better than the flesh'.[104] As with Paul's interpretation of the resurrection in I Corinthians 15, which was written to offer the only true understanding of it, so the Nag Hammadi Treatise was likewise written to a Gnostic who did not know what to believe. The anonymous author tells his recipient, a man named Rheginos, that the resurrection is a necessary experience for the Gnostic believer to undergo, but it is a raising from the death of ordinary consciousness to the life of *gnosis*:

> What, then, is the resurrection?... It is the truth which stands firm. It is the revelation of what is, and the transformation of things, and a transition into newness.[105]

The Gospel of Philip

The Gospel of Philip, one of the most stunningly original Nag Hammadi texts, corroborates this interpretation of the resurrection, advising the spiritual seeker 'while we are in this world it is best to acquire resurrection for ourselves'.[106] Philip is quite explicit about what the resurrection actually is:

> Those who say that the Lord died first and then rose up are in error, for he rose up first and then died. If one does not first attain the resurrection he will not die.[107]

The idea is reiterated later in the gospel, making it clear that the resurrection happens before death, not after it:

> Those who say they will die first and then rise are in error. If they do not first receive the resurrection while they live, when they die they will receive nothing.[108]

The notion of a resurrection of the flesh is rubbished, even appropriating Paul's argument for a resurrection of the body from I Corinthians 15:

> Some are afraid lest they rise naked, and they do not know that it is those who wear the flesh who are naked. It is those who unclothe themselves [i.e. attain *gnosis*] who are not naked. 'Flesh and blood shall not inherit the kingdom of God.'[109]

Like the Gospel of Thomas, the Gospel of Philip is a collection of sayings and parables, with the occasional narrative sequence. If the Gospel of Thomas is sometimes compared to Zen Buddhism,[110] the Gospel of Philip has something of the poetic enigma of the Taoist sage Chuang Tzu about it:

> The Lord went into the dye works of Levi and took seventy-two colours and threw them into a vat. He drew them out perfectly white. He said, 'In this way the earthly son has come as a dyer.'[111]

Furthering its similarities with Eastern philosophy, the gospel portrays this world as an illusion, where we 'stray from the real to the unreal'.[112] The contrast between the material plane and that of the Pleroma is described in a number of sayings, perhaps most beautifully in this one:

> Those who sow in winter reap in summer.
> Let us sow in the world to reap in summer.
> Winter is the world, summer the other realm.[113]

The way to assure one's path from the winter of this world into the unending summer of the true world is by acquiring the liberating *gnosis* that Jesus brings, and also by observing the sacraments of baptism, chrism, eucharist, redemption and the bridal chamber. This latter sacrament, as we have noted earlier, was generally regarded as the apogee of Gnostic experience and the Gospel of Philip mentions it on a number of occasions. Christ, according to Philip, is sent to heal the primordial rift between Adam and Eve:

> When Eve was in Adam there was no death.
> When she was cut from him,
> death came into being.
> If he enters what he was and takes her in him fully,
> death will disappear.[114]

What this appears to mean is that concepts such as 'man' and 'woman' need to be discarded in order to attain *gnosis*; there is only the receptive consciousness hungry for the truth and the physical body that consciousness occupies is completely immaterial. (A similar idea is expressed in Saying 114 of the Gospel of Thomas.)

But the Gospel of Philip is perhaps at its most striking in its poetry and the sometimes shocking images it presents us with:

God is a man-eater.[115]

Jesus came to crucify the world.[116]

In the world
humans make gods and worship their creation.
It would be better if the gods worshipped them![117]

Jesus tricked everyone. He did not appear as he was [...]
To the great he appeared as great,
To the small as small. To angels he appeared as an angel,
And to humans as human.[118]

These startling phrases reveal the Gnostics' love of poetry and metaphor. God does not, of course, literally eat people, but, once *gnosis* has been attained, one is effectively swallowed up in God, who will show no mercy once you have woken up. Jesus, likewise, will not appear to all people in the same way, simply because they have different capacities to understand the message of *gnosis*; therefore, for some people, he will appear as a child, for others, a fully grown adult teacher. In addition to these images, Philip tells us that Joseph made the cross on which his son was crucified and that Jesus, before bodily leaving this world, laughed at it in contempt.

Not all of the Gospel of Philip, though, is controversial in its imagery. Some of its poetry is beautiful:

A donkey turning a millstone walked a hundred miles.
When it was set loose, it found itself in the same place.
Some people travel long but go nowhere.
At twilight they have seen no cities or villages.[119]

There is water within water
and fire within chrism.[120]

The most contentious elements of Philip, however, are arguably those that deal with the nature of Christ, as well as one of the things that most irked the early Church, namely the recurring problem of women, and one woman in particular:

Three Marys walked with the Lord:
His mother, his sister, and Mary of Magdala,
His companion...[121]

The companion is Mary of Magdala. Jesus loved her
More than his students. He kissed her often
on her face, more than all his students,
And they said, 'Why do you love her more than us?'
The saviour answered them, saying to them,
'Why do I not love you like her?'[122]

The Gospel of Mary

The Gospel of Mary survives incomplete, having been discovered at Akhmim in Upper Egypt in 1896. The codex, which also contained the Apocryphon of John, the Sophia of Jesus Christ and a shortened version of the Act of Peter, was subsequently moved to Berlin, where it became known as the Berlin Codex. The Gospel of Mary falls into two distinct parts (indeed, they may have originally been two separate texts), with the first part showing the risen Christ teaching the disciples about the nature of sin. He tells the disciples that sin is not an ethical problem, but a cosmological one: sin came into being as a result of the improper mixing of the spiritual and material. He then instructs them to go and preach the gospel, reminding them not to be led astray by false teachers and to heed the gnosis that they already have: 'The Son of Man is within you. Follow him!'[123] In a typically Gnostic fashion, Jesus also tells them to 'not establish laws... so that you will not be bound by them'.[124] He then departs, leaving the disciples confused and upset, as they realise the dangers of preaching the gospel: 'If they did not spare him, how will they spare us?'[125]

This leads us into the second part of the gospel, in which Mary is portrayed as the woman whom Jesus loved more than other women and who was privy to secret knowledge. She encourages the disciples, seemingly taking over as leader of the group and reminding them that 'he prepared us and made us truly human', which 'turned their hearts to the good'.[126] Peter then asks Mary to tell them 'the words of the saviour that you remember, which you know and we do not', clearly showing that Mary is the one disciple whom Jesus entrusted with special teachings.

Mary then recounts a vision in which she encounters Jesus, who blesses her and tells her, 'where the mind is, there is the treasure',[127] words that give a decidedly Gnostic twist on Matthew 6:21 ('For where your treasure is, there will your heart be also'). Several pages are missing from the gospel at this point, and it picks up again with what is presumably a later stage of Mary's vision, in which the soul is portrayed as ascending, having shaken off the shackles of the body and earthly existence:

What binds me is slain, what surrounds me is destroyed, my desire is gone, ignorance is dead. In a world I was freed through another world, and in an image I was freed through a heavenly image. This is the fetter of forgetfulness that exists in the world of time. From now on I shall rest, through time, age, and aeon, in silence.'[128]

As soon as Mary finishes recounting her vision, the disciples start to argue amongst themselves. Andrew and Peter, in particular, can't believe that Mary's vision represents Jesus's teachings, their chauvinism being quite pronounced:

Peter also opposed her about all this. He asked the others about the saviour, 'Did he really speak to a woman secretly, without our knowledge, and not openly? Are we to turn and all listen to her? Did he prefer her to us?'[129]

Levi is the only disciple who comes to Mary's defence, arguing that if Jesus chose Mary, then Peter has no right to reject her. The argument fizzles out and the disciples go out to preach, although, as Karen L. King notes, 'the reader must wonder what kind of good news such proud and ignorant men will announce'.[130] As the Gospel of Mary shows, it is only Mary (and perhaps Levi) who have understood Jesus's teaching. Not only that, but the text 'affirms that her leadership of the other disciples is based upon superior spiritual understanding… the Gospel of Mary unreservedly supports the leadership of spiritually advanced women'.[131]

The Gnostic Feminine

The Gospel of Mary is not the only Gnostic text to champion the position and wisdom of women within the Gnostic community. Several Nag Hammadi tracts are voiced for women, or have female protagonists. One of the most striking examples is a text known as Thunder: Perfect Mind. The speaker is a woman who, while possibly not Sophia herself, has something of the youngest aeon about her:

> I was sent out from the power
> and have come to you who study me
> and am found by you who seek me.[132]

Possibly influenced by Jewish and Egyptian wisdom literature, the poem is a revelation discourse full of startling statements, many of them paradoxical:

> I am the first and the last.
> I am the honoured and the scorned.

I am the whore and the holy.
I am the wife and the virgin.
I am the mother and the daughter [...]
I am a silence incomprehensible
and an idea remembered often.
I am the voice whose sound is manifold
and word whose appearance is multiple.
I am the utterance of my name.[133]

Despite being something of an enigma among the Nag Hammadi texts — we do not know when or where it was written, nor by whom — it presents a powerful woman to the reader, 'an early instance of complete female empowerment, without apology or compromise'.[134] Elaine Pagels has suggested that works like Thunder: Perfect Mind reflect the fact that women enjoyed far greater status in Gnosticism than in orthodox Christianity:

Our evidence, then, clearly indicates a correlation between religious theory and social practice. Among such gnostic groups as the Valentinians, women were considered equal to men; some were revered as prophets; others acted as teachers, travelling evangelists, healers, priests, perhaps even bishops.[135]

Another Nag Hammadi text, the Exegesis on the Soul, depicts the soul as feminine ('she even has a womb') and recounts her descent into the world of matter after becoming separated from her father in the Pleroma. She inhabits a female body, where she is abused by a series of lovers and becomes a prostitute. Finally abandoned by the men who have defiled her, she becomes 'a poor desolate widow, helpless'. All of the children she has borne by her lovers are 'mute, blind and sickly. They are disturbed.'[136] (The soul's descent recalls the cosmology of Simon Magus, which saw the Ennoia descending into matter, where she ultimately became a prostitute, with Simon finding her wisdom in his own mystic consort, Helen.)

The text then breaks off from its narrative to cite the prophets Jeremiah, Hosea and Ezekiel on the subject of the prostitution of the soul, followed by St Paul from Ephesians: 'our struggle is not against flesh and blood... but against the world rulers of this darkness and the spirits of evil'.[137]

The father, sensing the soul's distress and desire for repentance, turns her womb inwards – it was originally outside of her – which has the effect of baptising and cleansing her. The father also sends the soul's brother down to her in order that she may be renewed in the mysteries of the bridal chamber. 'This marriage is not like a carnal marriage', the text tells us. 'In this marriage once they join they become a single life.'[138] The soul forgets her former partners and regains her true nature:

> The soul stirred. Her divine nature and her rejuvenation came from her father so she might return to where she was before. This is resurrection from the dead. This is ransom from captivity. This is the ascent to heaven.[139]

The text then urges the reader to repent through prayer, not by using our physical voices:

> ...but with the spirit, which is inside and comes from the depths, sighing, repenting for the life we led, confessing sins, recognising the deception we were in as shallow; perceiving the empty zeal; weeping over how we lived in darkness and in the wave; mourning for what we were so that he might pity us; hating ourselves for what we still are.[140]

In a classic example of a Gnostic writer supporting their argument through whatever sources they had access to, the Exegesis on the Soul finishes with quotes from Homer, showing Odysseus stranded on Calypso's island, longing to return home, and Helen lamenting being deceived by Aphrodite.

What does the Exegesis tell us about 'prostitution of the soul'? Like many Gnostic texts, it employs allegory, poetry and myth to convey its message. The prostituted soul could be likened to a person who has been led astray by various promises, or a spiritual seeker who latches onto the latest fads, desperate for liberation and happiness. A person, therefore, who ignores the latent *gnosis* within them.

Arguably more important than Thunder: Perfect Mind is a text known as Pistis Sophia (the title means 'faith-wisdom'). It was the most significant text to have surfaced prior to the Nag Hammadi discovery, having been found in Upper Egypt in 1784 by a British doctor named Askew. The British Museum bought it in 1795, whereafter it became known as the Askew Codex.[141] (A simpler, shorter version of the Pistis was later found at Nag Hammadi.)

Like the Gospel of Mary, Pistis Sophia takes place after the resurrection and features Mary Magdalene in a prominent role. The text tells us that Jesus has remained on earth for 11 years after the crucifixion to instruct the disciples, who believe that they have progressed far along the path of *gnosis* during this time, announcing:

> 'Blessed are we before all men who are on the earth, because the Saviour hath revealed this unto us, and we have received the Fullness and the total completion.'[142]

The disciples are, however, very much mistaken in their belief that they have received 'the total completion' (ch 2). Light descends over Jesus and he is taken up into heaven, which causes the disciples 'exceedingly great agitation' (ch 4). Upon Jesus's return, he informs them that 'I have gone to the regions out of which I had come forth', (ch 6) and promises to tell them everything 'from the beginning of the Truth unto its completion'.

The lengthy narrative Jesus relates concerns his journey 'upwards and inwards' and of his receiving a garment of light. He travels throughout the heavenly spheres, revealing the existence of the First Mystery – the true God – to the rulers of the spheres and their attendant angels. When he reaches the twelfth sphere, he encounters 'Adamas, the Great Tyrant', who tries to resist the light and, along with his minions, fights against it. Jesus cripples them all by taking a third of their power from them, and they 'were dashed down in the aeons and became as the inhabitants of the earth, dead and without breath of life' (ch 15).

It is at this point in Jesus's discourse that Mary Magdalene asks to speak. Jesus's reply clearly shows the esteem in which he holds her:

> And Jesus, the compassionate, answered and said unto Mary: 'Mary, thou blessed one, whom I will perfect in all mysteries of those of the height, discourse in openness, thou, whose heart is raised to the kingdom of heaven more than all thy brethren.'[143]

Mary interprets Jesus's narrative, describing how Isaiah prophesied what he has told them, then she begins to ask Jesus various questions; the only male disciple to quiz Jesus is Philip, who has been busy writing down Jesus's words. It is not so much the details of Mary's questions that are important here, rather the fact that she is taking the lead in asking Jesus to explain himself better, which suggests that she is actively assimilating Jesus's teachings, more so than the other, male, disciples (excepting Philip, possibly).

Jesus continues his discourse, revealing to the disciples that he encountered Pistis Sophia 'grieving and mourning, because she had not been admitted into the thirteenth aeon, her higher region' (ch 29). Pistis Sophia had originally been in the thirteenth aeon or sphere, but her longing for the First Mystery – the true God – had led her to neglect her aeonic duties. She is then tricked out of the thirteenth aeon by a rival, named Arrogant, who, together with other aeons, project their own light downwards. Pistis Sophia mistakes this light for the light of the First Mystery, heads towards it and becomes entrapped in the world of chaos and matter. She encounters Ialdabaoth, who strips her of her remaining power.

Pistis Sophia begins to sing hymns of repentance:

'Now, therefore, O Light of Truth, thou knowest that I have done this [descending from her aeon] in my innocence, thinking that the lion-faced light-power [Ialdabaoth] belonged to thee; and the sin which I have done is open before thee.

Suffer me no more to lack, O Lord, for I have had faith in thy light from the beginning; O Lord, O Light of the powers, suffer me no more to lack my light.

For because of thy inducement and for the sake of thy light am I fallen into this oppression, and shame hath covered me.

And because of the illusion of thy light, I am become a stranger to my brethren, the invisibles, and to the great emanations of Barbelo.'

Mary is once again allowed to interpret the story of Pistis Sophia, telling the disciples that what they have just heard was prophesied in Psalm 68. Jesus commends her interpretation and continues with a description of Pistis Sophia's second repentance. Once Jesus has finished speaking, Peter, clearly agitated by Mary's engagement with, and understanding of, the teaching, complains that 'We will not endure this woman, for she taketh the opportunity from us and hath let none of us speak, but she discourseth many times' (ch 36). Jesus lets Peter give his interpretation of the second repentance, while Martha is allowed to speak about the third repentance (there are thirteen in all). John interprets the fourth, at which point Philip complains that no one else is writing anything down; Jesus tells him that he has not finished his discourse yet, but also reminds Thomas and Matthew that they too have scribal duties.

Jesus continues to instruct the disciples, with each of them being allowed to interpret Jesus's words as they understand them. The rift between Mary and Peter, however, is made much more explicit later on. After being allowed to speak on several further occasions, Mary:

> ...came forwards and said: 'My Lord, my mind is ever under-standing, at every time to come forwards and set forth the solution of the words which she [Pistis Sophia] hath uttered; but I am afraid of Peter, because he threatened me and hateth our sex.'[144]

Jesus defends her right to speak, no doubt within earshot of Peter:

> 'Every one who shall be filled with the spirit of light to come for-wards and set forth the solution of what I say, no one shall be able to prevent him.'[145]

Peter, put in his place, shuts up[146] and Mary becomes, in the latter half of the text, the main questioner and interpreter of Jesus's words. Pistis Sophia is ultimately allowed to return to the thirteenth aeon, where she sings a song of praise to the First Mystery.

The second half of the text is taken up with further revelations, together with ethical instructions which the disciples are to preach once Jesus has returned to the light:

> 'Renounce love of the world, that ye may be worthy of the mysteries of the light and be saved from the pitch- and fire-coats of the dog-faced one.' (ch 102)

> 'Renounce wickedness, that ye may be worthy of the mysteries of the light and be saved from the fire-seas of Ariel.' (ch 102)

After giving a lengthy list of things to renounce, Jesus tells the disciples to encourage people to 'Be calm, that ye may receive the mysteries of the Light and go on high into the Light-kingdom.' Further exhortations follow, which bring together the orthodox and the Gnostic:

> 'Say unto them: Be ye loving-unto-men... Be ye gentle... Minister unto the poor and the sick and distressed... Be ye loving-unto-God, that ye may receive the mysteries of the Light and go on high into the Light-kingdom.'[147]

This is the nearest to orthodoxy that Pistis Sophia gets, as much of its length is occupied with cosmological writings and an exhaustive array of aeons, archons and mystical invocations. Later parts of the work deal with the afterlife states of the sinner and the reincarnational cycle that they must endure in order to be cleansed, with Jesus telling the disciples to urge people not to put off spiritual development for another lifetime, as the number of perfected souls could be reached at any moment. At this point, no more souls will be able to return to the Light-kingdom. This will be the end of time 'and the mystery of the First Mystery is completed, for the sake of which the universe hath arisen, that is: I am that Mystery.'[148]

The Laughing and Dancing Jesus

Jesus is portrayed in the canonical scriptures and later Christian art as the Man of Sorrows, and also as a man who apparently never laughed or smiled. Consequently, the Church has been a humourless place, with laughter being almost regarded as sinful.149 As we might expect from Gnostic authors, their version of Jesus is somewhat different. The Gospels of Thomas and Philip, two of the most striking Gnostic gospels, invite parallels with Eastern philosophies such as Buddhism and Taoism, but there are other Gnostic texts that portray Jesus in a rather more Hellenistic manner. To put it another way, some Gnostic texts seem to have been influenced by Graeco-Roman mystery schools, and therefore the Jesus they portray has accordingly more in common with the priesthood of a mystery religion.

The Acts of John, a Greek version of which was discovered at Oxyrhynchus in the 1890s, could have been composed some time in the second century, with some traditions holding that the Gnostic chronicler Leucius Charinus was its author, although this attribution isn't certain.[150] Leucius was said to have been a young disciple of the aged St John, from whom he received secret teachings and stories about Jesus. The Acts of John is an account of the activities of the apostle in Asia Minor some time after the crucifixion, its most celebrated passage being the so-called 'Round Dance of the Cross'. This scene takes the form of a sermon delivered by John to a crowd of people, probably in Ephesus, where much of the Acts of John takes place. John recounts the events of the night before Jesus was arrested. In canonical accounts, Jesus prays in the Garden of Gethsemane, but in the Acts of John,[151] he instead commands them to dance and respond with an 'Amen' to his praises to God:

> He then began to sing a hymn, and to say:
> 'Glory be to you, Father!'
> And we circling him said, 'Amen'
> 'Glory be to you, Word! Glory be to you, Grace!'
> 'Amen' [...]
> We praise you, O Father. We give thanks to you, light, in whom darkness does not abide.'
> 'Amen.'[152]

As the disciples continue to respond to Jesus, he begins to dance and instructs them to do the same:
> 'The whole universe takes part in the dancing.'
> 'Amen'

'He who does not dance, does not know what is being done.'
'Amen'

Jesus's hymn now becomes a series of paradoxes, stating that he will flee and stay, adorn and be adorned, unite and be united. The hymn ends with some beautiful mystical statements:

'I am a lamp to you who see me.'
'Amen.'
'I am a mirror to you who perceive.'
'Amen.'
'I am a door to you who knock on me.'
'Amen.'
'I am a way to you, wayfarer.'
'Amen.'

Jesus then encourages the disciples to understand the dance by seeing him within themselves, which echoes the Gospel of Philip's statement that those who have achieved *gnosis* are 'no longer a Christian, but Christ,'[153] and also the Gospel of Thomas, in which Jesus declares:

'Whoever drinks from my mouth will become like me.
I myself shall become that person,
and the hidden things will be revealed to that one.'[154]

The similarity with the mystery schools is made explicit in the very next line, in which Jesus enjoins the disciples to 'keep silence about my mysteries!' Jesus explains that, through the mystery of the suffering that he is about to undergo, the disciples will have the chance to become moved and, in doing so, will be 'moved to become wise... Learn suffering and you shall have the power not to suffer.'[155]

Following the Round Dance comes a section known as the Revelation of the Mystery of the Cross. When Jesus is crucified, the disciples 'fled all ways', with John hiding in a cave on the Mount of Olives. While he is there, Jesus appears to him and shows him a cross made of light around which a multitude stands. The cross is the Word which unites all things and only when people hearken to it will all the light particles scattered within humanity be gathered back together again and be taken up. Jesus also tells John that he is not 'he who is upon the cross' at Calvary, reflecting the common Gnostic belief that Jesus was a divine being, not a human one. Furthermore, Jesus informs John that:

'You hear that I suffered, yet I suffered not; that I suffered not, yet I did suffer; that I was pierced, yet I was not wounded; hanged, and I was not hanged, that blood flowed from me, yet it did not flow.'[156]

The Nag Hammadi Apocalypse of Peter[157] takes the image of a Christ who does not suffer during the crucifixion one stage further, portraying Jesus as 'glad and laughing on the tree'.[158] Jesus explains to Peter that:

'He whom you saw on the tree, glad and laughing, this is the living Jesus. But this one into whose hands and feet they drive the nails is his fleshly part, which is the substitute being put to shame, the one who came into being in his likeness. But look at him, and look at me.'[159]

The idea of a fleshy Jesus being crucified while the real Jesus laughs would be more than enough to have the Church Fathers reaching for their smelling salts; it completely subverts orthodox doctrine. Subversion, however, was not the Gnostic intention. Rather, they held that the crucifixion – like the rest of Jesus's ministry and teaching – can only really be understood through paradox, poetry and startling images. The concept of the laughing Jesus is perhaps best understood this way. Timothy Freke and Peter Gandy point out that, while the world is full of beauty, it is also full of suffering and death. The way to free oneself is through gnosis (which they term 'lucid living'), which in turn enables one to both rise above suffering and empathise with those who are experiencing it:

> ...when we live lucidly we find ourselves loving all and suffering willingly with all. This is the state of gnosis symbolised by the sublime figure of the laughing Jesus.[160]

The Gospel of Judas

If the Gnostics could regard the Serpent in the Garden of Eden as wise and benign, and Jesus as a teacher who laughs and dances, then it really should come as no surprise that Judas Iscariot, long regarded as one of the most detested figures in the history of Western civilisation, was a revered figure for some Gnostic groups, such as the Cainites. The Gospel of Judas was long thought lost, our only knowledge of it coming from Irenaeus, who wrote that the Cainites:

> ...declare that Judas the traitor was thoroughly acquainted with these things [gnosis], and that he alone, knowing the truth as no others did, accomplished the mystery of the betrayal; by him all things, both earthly and heavenly, were thus thrown into confusion. They produce a fictitious history of this kind, which they style the Gospel of Judas.[161]

Another Church Father, Epiphanius of Salamis, complained that the Gospel of Judas held Christ's betrayer in high esteem, as someone who had 'performed a good work for our salvation'.[162]

At a press conference in 2004, however, it was announced that the gospel may have at last been found. As with the Nag Hammadi library, the discovery of which included murder, black market dealings and texts being smuggled out of Egypt, so the discovery of the Gospel of Judas was a saga of underhand dealings, theft and academic wrangling. It appears that a codex (since christened Codex Tchacos) was discovered in 1978 in a cave near the village of Maghagha, which lies about 120 miles south of Cairo. As at Nag Hammadi, the discovery was made by locals who, although illiterate, knew that it was written in Coptic and that they could find a good price for the old book on the antiquities market. The codex was sold to an Egyptian dealer named Hanna, who tried without success to find a buyer. Even worse, the codex was stolen from him in 1982 and he had to travel to Europe, where he suspected it had been sold, to look for it. The codex was eventually recovered and offered for sale to American coptologists in Geneva in 1983. When the Americans arrived, they found the codex in reasonable condition and noted that it contained Gnostic texts. However, the asking price – $50,000 – was deemed to be too much and the Americans went home. Hanna put the codex in a safe-deposit box in Hicksville, New York, where it apparently remained for the next 17 years. The codex was finally sold in 2001 and on 24 July of that year was provisionally identified as the Gospel of Judas. However, the codex had deteriorated greatly in its 17-year sojourn in the safe-deposit box, with the result that a great deal of work had to be done to prevent it from crumbling away altogether. A translation finally appeared in 2006.[163]

Now that the gospel is widely available, it can be seen that Irenaeus was in fact quite right when he described the Gospel of Judas as portraying Judas as 'thoroughly acquainted' with Gnostic teachings, and that 'he alone, knowing the truth as no others did, accomplished the mystery of the betrayal'. According to this gospel, Judas is Christ's best and most loyal disciple, who is the only one of the 12 to understand precisely who Jesus is:

> Judas said to him, 'I know who you are and where you have come from. You are from the immortal realm of Barbelo. And I am not worthy to utter the name of the one who has sent you.'[164]

Although mainly comprised of a long discourse between Jesus and Judas, the Gospel of Judas does have a small amount of narrative, in that the events it depicts are said to have taken place 'three days before he celebrated Passover'.[165] The disciples are celebrating the eucharist, when Jesus laughs at them. When questioned, Jesus replies that the disciples are unwittingly praising the creator God, not the true God. This makes the disciples angry and they 'began blaspheming against him in their hearts'.[166] Judas then makes his 'immortal realm of Barbelo' comment to Jesus and is taken aside for private instruction in 'the mysteries of the kingdom'.

Next day, Jesus appears again to the disciples, who report that they have all dreamt of the temple in Jerusalem. In the dream, the priests keep people waiting at the altar and sacrifice their own wives and children, all the while maintaining a false piety. This seems to be an attack on the emerging orthodoxy in Christianity; Jesus tells the disciples to have nothing to do with it. He reassures them, saying: 'Each of you has his own star', a possible reference to Plato, who believed that if a person lived well, at their death they would return to the star that had been assigned to them.[167]

Judas seems to have been the only one not to have had this dream. Instead, he tells Jesus that he has had a vision in which the other disciples were stoning him. Judas is worried that he is under the control of the archons, but Jesus reassures him, telling him that he will progress spiritually far more than the other disciples. A cosmological discourse follows, in which the true God creates the aeons and angels. One of the angels, Saklas (an alternative name for Ialdabaoth, meaning 'fool'), then creates humanity. Judas asks Jesus about human destiny, but Jesus tells him not to worry, as Saklas and his archons will one day be destroyed 'when Saklas completes the span of time assigned for him'.[168]

It is when Judas asks about what the baptised should do that Jesus reveals Judas's true destiny. Those who offer sacrifices to Saklas –

probably a reference to those who participate in orthodox Christianity – are inferior to Judas, who 'will exceed all of them. For you will sacrifice the man that clothes me'.[169] In other words, Jesus is essentially asking Judas to betray him in order to liberate the true Jesus from his mortal body, the 'man that clothes me'. After this, Jesus reassures Judas that 'the star that leads the way is your star', and Judas is transfigured in a luminous cloud, suggesting that he has attained a higher state of spiritual development than the other disciples.

The gospel ends with Judas carrying out Jesus's request: he betrays his master to the high priests. The setting is not the Garden of Gethsemane as in the canonical gospels, but what seems to be the room where the Last Supper was celebrated.[170] The high priests are nervous of causing a disturbance when arresting Jesus, as there are supporters in the vicinity, and 'he was regarded by all as a prophet'. The final moments of the gospel have all the pared-down piety of a Bresson film:

> They [the high priests] approached Judas and said to him, 'What are you doing here? You are Jesus's disciple.'
> Judas answered them as they wished. And he received some money from them and handed him over to them.[171]

The crucifixion is not shown; neither is Judas's suicide. Indeed, on the basis of his dream earlier in the gospel, it would seem that the other disciples tried to stone Judas to death. Whether he suffered any inner turmoil in betraying his master is likewise left for us to wonder. The text simply shows Judas, Jesus's most trusted and loyal disciple, carrying out his master's last wish.

The Council of Nicaea and the Letter of Athanasius

By the time the Gospel of Judas was written, possibly in the late second century, the lines between Gnosticism and orthodoxy were becoming ever more firmly drawn. The process of establishing what constituted orthodoxy was a long and slow process, and for many decades it was difficult to separate the Gnostics from the orthodox. Gnostics such as the Valentinians regarded themselves as Christians and couldn't understand why their beliefs provoked such wrath amongst the likes of Irenaeus. For a time, the lines between heresy and orthodoxy were sufficiently vague to allow certain Church Fathers to express ideas which took them close to Gnosticism. Clement of Alexandria and Origen are perhaps the most important in this respect. Clement described a true *gnosis* and a false *gnosis* in his writings, seeing the true Gnostic living life in oneness with God.

> The life of the Gnostic is, in my view, no other than works and words which correspond to the tradition of the Lord.[172]

Origen stressed the importance of knowledge over faith, and held that the soul was pre-existent and had fallen into matter but would one day return to God. Such heterodox thinking was frowned upon, however, and Origen endured a period later in life when he was regarded as a heretic.

When Christianity became legalised in the Roman Empire in 313, it was only a matter of time before the champions of orthodoxy – the spiritual descendants of Irenaeus, Hippolytus and Tertullian – would be required to bring their religion into line with the Emperor Constantine's overhaul of the Empire. Some sort of attempt at defining orthodoxy would have probably happened anyway, as the various factions within Christianity were not seeing eye to eye on various doctrinal matters. The Arian school, in particular, was proving to be controversial, with its view that God the Father and Christ the Son were two distinct entities, with Christ being seen as inferior to God.

To settle the matter, Constantine convened the Council of Nicaea, whose opening session began on 20 May 325. In the two months that the Council sat, the 300 or so Church Fathers gathered at Nicaea debated a number of topics, including the fixing of the date of Easter, but by far the most important issue was Arianism. In an attempt to establish an orthodox position on Christ's divine nature, the Nicene Creed was promulgated on 19 June, which drew the battle lines between the orthodox and everyone else. Belief in the tenets of the Creed were central to orthodoxy. They included belief in 'God, the Father... maker of heaven and earth', in Christ 'the only Son of God... eternally begotten of the Father, true God from true God, begotten, not made, one in Being with the Father', who 'was born of the Virgin Mary and became man. For our sake he was crucified under Pontius Pilate; he suffered, died, and was buried. On the third day he rose again in fulfilment of the Scriptures'. Christ's flock was to be ministered unto solely by 'one holy catholic and apostolic Church'.[173] The key issue of Christ's divinity and his position as 'one in Being with the Father' was settled by vote. The Arians lost and were declared heretics. The Church was sending out a clear message: they were the only means by which one could achieve salvation.

Once orthodoxy in terms of belief had been established, a canon was not long in following. The Patriarch of Alexandria, Athanasius, an opponent of Arianism, was the first person to list, in his Easter letter of 367, the same New Testament books that we still know today. Known as Athanasius's 39th Festal Letter, it condemned heretics and their 'apocryphal books to which they attribute antiquity and give the name of saints'.[174] As a result, book-burning became widespread, the most notorious example being the burning of the great library at Alexandria in 391.[175]

A copy of Athanasius's letter, in Coptic translation, found its way to one of the monasteries founded by St Pachomius near Nag Hammadi. While we don't know if the books that make up the Nag Hammadi library all came from one monastery or from a group of them, it is probable that the texts had been copied out and used by Gnostic elements within the Pachomian monastic movement. With the arrival of the letter, however, both the texts and their copyists were now very clearly under threat. Preferring not to destroy the books, the monks had only one choice open to them: the 13 codices that make up the Nag Hammadi library were sealed into a large red earthenware jar and buried for posterity at the base of the cliffs at Jabal al-Tarif. Some of the texts may even have been freshly copied before being hidden, as the Gospel of the Egyptians concludes with a reference to being buried in a mountain:

> The Great Seth wrote this book... He placed it in the mountain that is called Charaxio, in order that, at the end of the times and the eras... it may come forth and reveal this incorruptible, holy race of the great saviour, and those who dwell with them in love, and the great, invisible eternal Spirit, and his only begotten Son, and the eternal light... and the incorruptible Sophia... and the whole Pleroma in eternity. Amen.[176]

None of the monks could have realised, on the day the books were buried, that the codices would indeed one day come forth, 'at the end of the times and the eras'. But for now, they were buried under the sands of Egypt, seemingly forever.

Influence and Legacy

The burial of the texts at Nag Hammadi did not signal the end of Gnosticism, as various Gnostic movements were still active. Perhaps the most important of them at this stage was Manichaeism.

To the Church, Manichaeism was the deadliest of heresies, even worse than Marcionism. That Manichaeism enjoyed widespread popularity in the West is evinced by the fact that St Augustine of Hippo was a Listener of the sect for nine years. When the preaching of St Ambrose and an epiphany in a garden in Milan turned Augustine towards Christianity in 386, he denounced Manichaeism in *De Manichaeis* and *De Heresibus*, which were to become the Church's standard reference books on all matters heretical and were frequently used in order to identify suspected heretics. To Augustine, his former faith was a perversion of the truth of the gospels, and its missionaries and priests were deceitful and cunning.

With Augustine its most vocal and authoritative opponent, Manichaeism began to go into decline. As early as 372, Manicheans were forbidden from congregating and the Roman emperor, Theodosius I (379–5) – who made Christianity the state religion in 380 – passed legislation against them. The fifth and sixth centuries saw a concerted effort by Rome to wipe out Mani's followers, while similar measures were enacted in the Byzantine Empire. Early in his reign, the Byzantine Emperor Justinian the Great (527–65) introduced the death penalty for Manichaeans, the favoured method of despatching adherents of the Religion of Light being burning. So effective was the persecution under Justinian that, by the time of his death in 565, Manichaeism had been effectively wiped out altogether in the West. The Church was tightening its grip.[177]

Manichaeism might have been extinguished from Europe, but the name lived on as a byword for a dualist, heretic or merely a political opponent.[178] Many Manichaeans were forced to travel eastwards to escape the persecution, resulting in the religion spreading throughout central Asia, Tibet and China. In some places Manichaeism was outlawed, such as in T'ang China, where a massive wave of anti-Manichaean persecution was launched around 843, but in other areas it thrived. The Uighur Empire (roughly modern north-west China), for instance, adopted Manichaeism as the state religion in 764, which it remained as until the Mongol invasions of the thirteenth century. In 1292, Marco Polo encountered Manichaeans in the Fukien province of China, and it is here that they survived the longest, holding out against further waves of persecution until the early seventeenth century.[179]

Despite the Church's success in killing off (frequently literally) Manichaeism, Gnosticism returned to haunt the Church once more during the High Middle Ages, a threat that became known as the Great Heresy.

The Great Heresy

As Europe sank into the Dark Ages, what vestiges of Gnosticism that were left seem to have gone largely underground, if they were not extirpated altogether. The legacy of Gnosticism during this period is largely that of dualist groups such as the Massalians and the Paulicians,[180] who may have influenced the rise of what, to the mediaeval Church, was the greatest threat it had faced since the days of Marcion: the Great Heresy of the Bogomils and the Cathars. These groups were the same in essence, so we will examine them as one phenomenon.

The Bogomils emerged from the gloom of Dark Age Bulgaria in the early years of the tenth century. No one knows precisely where the Bogomils came from. They are first recorded during the reign of the Bulgarian tsar, Peter (927–69), who was forced to write twice during the 940s to the patriarch of Constantinople, Theophylact Lecapenus, asking for help against the new heresy. Theophylact was known to be a man more at home in the stable than the cathedral, but he did have time enough to declare Bogomilism to be a mixture of Manichaeism and Paulicianism. A serious riding accident prevented him from giving Peter more help and the new dualist faith continued to grow at an alarming rate; so much so that a Bulgarian priest known as Cosmas was forced to denounce the new sect in his Sermon Against the Heretics, written at the very end of Peter's reign (it was certainly completed by 972).

Cosmas writes that the sect was founded by a priest named Bogomil, but there is both controversy over what his name means, and whether it was his real name at all. Some interpret Bogomil as meaning 'beloved of God', while others opt for 'worthy of God's mercy' and 'one who entreats God'. Cosmas describes the Bogomils as rejecting the Old Testament and Church sacraments; the only prayer they used being the Lord's Prayer. They did not venerate Icons or relics, while the cross was denounced as the instrument of Christ's torture. The Church itself was seen as being in league with the devil, whom they regarded as not only the creator of the visible world, but also as Christ's brother. Their priests were strict ascetics, abstaining from meat, wine and marriage.

Like many strands of Gnosticism before them, the Bogomils were – at least initially – moderate dualists, and also, like their Gnostic forebears, they interpreted canonical scripture in their own, idiosyncratic way. They knew the scriptures inside out, but what puzzled Cosmas was the way in which they interpreted them. For instance, in the Parable of the Prodigal Son (Luke 15.11–32), they saw the elder, stay-at-home son as being Christ, while the younger, prodigal, son was Satan. As with most strands of Gnosticism, the Bogomils were Docetic, that is to say, they regarded Christ's earthly body as an apparition, which meant that he didn't really suffer on the cross, but only appeared to, which recalls the 'glad and laughing' Jesus of the Nag Hammadi scriptures.

The Bogomil church was divided into two main classes, the Perfect and the Believers, similar to the Manichaean system of Elect and Listeners, although the Bogomils apparently did have a Listener class as well, who were below the Believers. According to the monk Euthymius of Constantinople, who was writing in about 1050, the Bogomil Listener became a Believer by way of a baptism which included the initiate having the gospel placed on their head, while the actual baptism itself was done, not by water, which, like the rest of the material world, was regarded as Satanic, but by the laying-on of hands. The road from Believer to Perfect was a long and arduous one, with intensive teachings, ascetic practices and study that took two years or more to complete. The ceremony in which a Believer became a Perfect was similar to that which made a Listener a Believer, and was known as the *consolamentum* (the consoling), or *baptisma*. For Euthymius, it was 'whole heresy and madness' and 'unholy service to the devil and his mysteries';[181] the Bogomils, however, regarded themselves as being the heirs to true, apostolic Christianity. Modelling themselves on Christ and the Apostles, Bogomil leaders had 12 disciples and lived lives of simplicity and poverty, in reaction to what they saw as the irredeemable corruption and false teachings of the Church.

What further worried Euthymius was that the Bogomils seemed to be a fully developed counter-church, one whose missionaries were active in spreading the word of the heretical faith. How, when and where the Bogomils organised is still a matter of debate, but it seems that, right from the time they were noted during Tsar Peter's reign, they were already a distinct group, with their own teachings. Again, whether they were influenced by Paulicianism, Manichaeism or even Zoroastrianism is a matter of conjecture, but one thing is certain: their missionaries were very active and travelled westwards, where they began gaining converts in the Rhineland, northern Italy, the Low Countries and France.

In the West, the heresy became known as Catharism, from the Greek word *katharos*, meaning 'pure'.[182] The first Cathars known in the West were discovered at Cologne in 1143, where a group of them blew their cover by arguing over a point of doctrine. Hauled up before the bishop of Cologne, it was discovered that the Cathar church was organised into a three-tier system of Listeners, Elect and Believers, showing the direct influence of the Bogomils and the Manichaeans. They practised the Bogomil form of baptism, condemned marriage and 'had a very large number of adherents scattered throughout the world'. The Cathars told the bishop that they had 'lain concealed from the time of the martyrs even to their own day [1143]'.[183] Most of the Cologne Cathars were persuaded to come back to the Church, although two of their number remained unrepentant; they were seized by a mob and burnt.

The Cathars, or Good Christians as they called themselves, inherited much from the Bogomils. Like them, the Cathar faith was dualist, holding that the material world is evil, the creation of the devil himself. The true God existed in a world of eternal light beyond the dark abyss of human existence. Both the Cathars and the Bogomils completely rejected the Church and all its sacraments, regarding it as the church of Satan. The only sacrament they observed was the *consolamentum*, which served as baptism or, if administered on the death-bed, extreme unction. The only prayer both churches used was the Lord's Prayer, with the Cathars substituting 'supersubstantial bread' for 'daily bread'. Both Bogomils and Cathars alike rejected most of the Old Testament – and its God – as Satanic.[184] Both movements regarded the entity of the Church – Catholic in the West, Orthodox in the East – as the church of Satan, rejecting it utterly. Church buildings – the churches, chapels and cathedrals themselves – were likewise seen as no more holy than any other building; neither sect built any, preferring instead to meet in people's homes, or in barns or fields. The Cross was seen as the instrument of Christ's torture, and Bogomils and Cathars alike refused to venerate it. They interpreted the eucharist allegorically and took the Docetic line on Christ's nature, his miracles, passion and resurrection. Cathars and Bogomils alike regarded marriage as fornication, a means by which further souls could be entrapped in matter through the thoroughly distasteful business of childbirth. While there is little or no evidence regarding women in the Bogomil church, the Cathars looked upon women as being the equal of men, with Catharism offering women the chance to participate fully in the faith at all levels.

The structure of the Cathar church was again derived from the Bogomil model. Cathars were divided into three classes: Listeners, Believers and Perfect. The Listeners were people who chose not to commit to the faith wholeheartedly; they might hear the occasional sermon, but no more. At this stage, Listeners would hear sermons that were close in spirit to evangelical Christianity. If they chose to become a Believer, they would be asked to participate in a ceremony known as the *convenanza*, which formally bound them to the Cathar church. Believers formed the majority of the movement. They were ordinary men and women who had ordinary jobs and lived in towns or villages. They were not cut off in monastic seclusion, did not have to abstain from meat, wine or sex, but were very much involved in the world of matter. They were taught to be in the world, but not of it, to follow the basic teachings of the gospels, to love one another, to live a life of faith and to seek God. They were generally not exposed to dualist doctrine, which was nearly always reserved for the ears of the Perfect alone. The Perfect were the austere, top-level Cathars who were effectively the movement's priesthood. Both Cathars and Bogomils held the Perfect in the highest regard: they were seen as embodying the Holy Spirit, being the living church itself. They were seen by the faithful as nothing less than 'living icons'.[185]

The Church, alarmed at the spread and popularity of Catharism, tried to reason with them. A series of public debates was held in the Languedoc, where Catharism was particularly strong, between the years 1204 and 1206. The Cathars held their ground. Given their popularity, obvious moral integrity (a fact which the Church was forced to acknowledge, its own priests at the time being noticeably rather lax in this area), and the political support of many of the Languedoc's nobility, the Church realised that getting rid of them would take little short of a crusade. Which is precisely what happened.

Launched in 1209, the Albigensian Crusade (named after the town of Albi, one of the Cathars' strongholds) was a Church-sponsored crime against humanity. Even by mediaeval standards, the sheer level of barbarity, cruelty and callousness is not only shocking today, but even shocked Church apologists at the time, who often put the violence down to the actions of hard-to-control mercenaries. This was not the case: the atrocities were ordered from on high, from the papal legate in the area, and also from the crusade's psychopathic leader, Simon de Montfort. Whole towns were put to the sword whether they were Cathar or not; mass burnings were commonplace. Things went into respite somewhat after de Montfort was killed in 1218 while besieging Toulouse, but the complicated tangle of Languedocian politics eventually brought in the French crown. The local nobility didn't stand a chance against the powerful northern armies, and the crusade officially ended with a southern capitulation in 1229. The Cathars continued a precarious existence in their Pyrenean castles as the 1230s saw the creation of the Inquisition to root them out. Finally, the last major Cathar stronghold at Montségur fell in March 1244; all 225 Cathar Perfect were burnt at the stake. Although the faith continued largely underground until the 1320s (and the 1380s in Italy), 1244 marked the end of Catharism as a major force.

It could be argued that Catharism was not properly gnostic, in that its tenets stressed the importance of receiving the *consolamentum* over *gnosis*. Being consoled would save a Believer, not *gnosis*, but it could also be argued that, without receiving the liberating *gnosis* that this world was created by the devil and is therefore not our true home, there would be no reason to become consoled. It is almost an academic point. Catharism did share much else in common with the Gnostics of antiquity and its brutal extermination is a reminder, if any were needed, of how far Gnosticism and organised religion remained apart.

Troubadours and Alchemists

Despite the best efforts of the Church to eradicate heresy, traces of Gnostic thought are also detectable elsewhere during the time of the Cathars and on into the later Middle Ages. The troubadours were wandering minstrels who flourished alongside the Cathars and were often closely connected to them through family ties. They would travel from one royal or noble court to the next, singing songs of love which often idealised women.[186] (They also flourished in Germany, where they were known as Minnesingers.) Their songs and poems developed what became known as courtly love (from which we get the term 'courting'). This was a highly formalised kind of wooing, in which the act of love became the highest state to which one could hope to attain. Whilst scholars still debate the extent to which the troubadours may – or may not – have been gnostically inclined, 'there is no *prima facie* evidence that they were not Cathar sympathisers'.[187] We should therefore note a number of interesting parallels.

The troubadours, like the Cathars and the Gnostics of classical antiquity, regarded women as the equal of men; indeed, some of their most notable patrons were Cathar women such as Esclarmonde of Foix. Marriage was likewise frowned upon. In terms of Christian orthodoxy, the troubadours were tricksters, anti-Church and never slow to mock clerical failings.[188] Perhaps most tellingly, there is in their work a sense of purification, of a higher world attainable through love and devotion, a 'generally upward spiritual aspiration: the development of consciousness.'[189] In some of their songs there are 'the signs of a dualism of higher and lower worlds, spirit and matter, light and darkness';[190] in allegorical terms, the idealised lady of the troubadours' songs could be seen as none other than Sophia herself. Indeed, the troubadours could be said to have borne witness to the divine feminine, a complement to the Cathars' bearing witness to 'the archetype of the numinous *self*, the divine man within (the Christ-*Lapis* = stone, hidden from consciousness) who comes into this world from the dominion of heaven'.[191]

Christ as a hidden stone is a concept that would certainly not have been lost on practitioners of the Middle Ages' other great Gnostic stream, alchemy. As we have seen, Hermeticism (the philosophy that underpins alchemy) can be counted among the main non-Christian forms of Gnosticism. Alchemy, on the other hand, used a great deal of Christian symbolism and many of the first major alchemists in Europe were also churchmen – bishops, abbots and friars. (One, Albertus Magnus, even became a saint, whilst another, Gerbert d'Aurillac, became Pope Sylvester II.) One does not need to look very closely at alchemical texts, however, to see that alchemists were using the framework of Christianity for their own ends. Christ was associated with the goal of alchemy, the production of the Philosopher's Stone, whilst various Old Testament figures such as Noah and Elijah were seen as alchemical adepts. The Book of Genesis held a particular fascination for alchemists and stories were interpreted as allegories of the alchemical path: God's creation of the world from chaos was seen as the ultimate alchemical act, whilst the work itself was said to take place in the alchemist's *terra adamica*, the 'earth of Adam', a reference to the first man, Adam.

When we understand what the 'earth of Adam' actually is, we realise that alchemy was not the futile quest to turn lead into gold, but something far more Gnostic: the *terra adamica* is nothing other than the alchemist's own body. Any changes that took place in the laboratory were thought to be reflections of changes in the alchemist's own being. The true transmutation was not that of base metals into gold, but of the alchemist becoming a 'living philosophical stone' – in other words, acquiring *gnosis*. In a further echo of gnostic thought, the great work was overseen by Sophia herself, in the guise of Lady Alchymia.

The Gnostic Renaissance

The end of Catharism did not spell the end of Gnosticism. A major turning point in its fortunes came in 1452, when Constantinople fell to the Turks. This precipitated a huge exodus of scholars and priests, many of whom carried with them priceless manuscripts that had never been seen in the West. Amongst the texts that arrived in Europe was the *Corpus Hermeticum*, which came to the attention of Cosimo de Medici. Cosimo, apart from being the Pope's banker, was passionately interested in the new learning that was beginning to sweep Europe and he ordered the scholar Marsilio Ficino to abandon his then work-in-progress, a translation of the complete works of Plato, in favour of translating the Hermetic texts.

The impact of these Gnostic texts is difficult to overstate; in places such as Florence, where the Renaissance was flourishing, it was little short of revolutionary. In general, Renaissance philosophy tends towards celebrating both man and the world, rather than regarding them as a prison for the spirit. Human nature is seen as having an innate dualism to it, namely that it can be the arena for developing the divinity within oneself through conscious choice, or, if one does not choose to develop the divine spark within one, then human nature – the whole person – stagnates. The Poimandres, one of the Hermetic texts translated by Ficino, urges:

> ...why do you delay? Seeing that you have received all, why do you not make yourself a guide to those who are worthy of the boon, so that mankind may through you be saved by God?[192]

This sense of both the urgent need for human renewal and the inherent optimism of its possibility, informs what is perhaps the most celebrated example of Gnostic influence during this period, Pico della Mirandola's *Oration on the Dignity of Man*. Pico was a young and brilliant scholar, the Mozart of Renaissance Humanism and his short life – he was dead at 31 – was nothing if not eventful: he knew Ficino personally and enjoyed the patronage of Cosimo de Medici. His magnum opus, the 900 theses addressed to the scholars of Europe, mingled Gnostic, Christian, Aristotelian, Kabbalistic and Neoplatonic thought into what was more or less the manifesto of the Renaissance. The *Oration* was added to the Theses as an introduction to the whole work. Gnostic sympathies, however, tie both the Theses and the *Oration* together:

> Exalted to a lofty height, we shall measure therefrom all things that are and shall be and have been in indivisible eternity; and, admiring their original beauty, full of divine power we shall no longer be ourselves but shall become He Himself Who made us.

For he who knows himself in himself knows all things, as Zoroaster first wrote. When we are finally lighted in this knowledge, we shall in bliss be addressing the true Apollo on intimate terms... And, restored to health, Gabriel 'the strength of God', shall abide in us, leading us through the miracles of nature and showing us on every side the merit and the might of God. [193]

For Pico and those that came after him, man was nothing less than a magus and therefore a potential god.

Gnosticism and magic have had a long association, going back to the days of Simon Magus, who was not only the first Gnostic, but was also seen as a magician. His detractors, and there were many, regarded him as a charlatan and 'messenger of the devil',[194] but this may very well be the fledgling Church's inability to understand magic, which was always seen as 'black'. In fact, there is no such thing, only a power that can be used for either selfless or selfish purposes (which has been misrepresented as 'white' and 'black' magic respectively). If Simon practised magic, therefore, it was likely to be intimately related to spiritual practice – using magic as a way of appeasing the archons and supplicating the aeons. 'Magic is about power,' as Stuart Holroyd notes, 'and power derives from knowledge.'[195] Any means of acquiring the knowledge that will free us, including magical knowledge and practice, is therefore to be welcomed.

Magic, and the concept of man as magus, resurfaced in the Renaissance. Ficino, after translating the Hermetic Corpus and Plato, wrote tracts of 'natural' (or what popular culture today may regard as 'white') magic, as did many major figures in the century that followed him, including Cornelius Agrippa, Paracelsus, John Dee, Giordano Bruno and Jacob Boehme. For all of them, knowledge free from the stifling shackles of the Church was the key to salvation.

The Gnostic Enlightenment

The so-called Age of Enlightenment saw the growth of intellectual freedom. Although Bruno had been burnt as an impenitent heretic in 1600 and Galileo forced by the Inquisition to recant his own work in 1633, in the following century Gibbon and Voltaire published works that, in a previous era, could well have seen them joining Bruno at the stake. In The Decline and Fall of the Roman Empire, Gibbon wrote that 'The Gnostics were distinguished as the most polite, the most learned and the most wealthy of the Christian name,' whose beliefs, while 'obscure' were 'sublime'.[196] Gibbon's revisionism is 'if not an advertisement for heresy, then [is] at least a subversion of orthodoxy'.[197] Although Gibbon may have been playing devil's advocate in showing sympathy for the Gnostics, the same could not be said for his great contemporary, Voltaire.

In his book *Candide*, Voltaire satirises the Enlightenment belief that 'all is for the best in this best of possible worlds'. The eponymous hero suffers a series of misfortunes, with Voltaire suggesting that the only character who sees the world aright (or at least as Voltaire himself does) is the itinerant scholar Martin, who introduces himself to Candide as a Manichaean. Candide replies there are no longer any Manichaeans left in the world, to which Martin replies that he can't see the world in any other way, explaining that:

> 'The devil is so involved in the affairs of this world that he may well be in me, as he is everywhere else; but when I consider this globe, or rather globule, I think that God must have abandoned it to some evil being.'

Voltaire's story 'Plato's Dream' also shows his sympathy with Gnostic ideas. The narrative recounts how the Demiurge, after having 'peopled the infinite spaces of the innumerable worlds', arranges a contest for the archons. One, called Démogorgon, is given 'the bit of mud that is called earth', and he creates out of it the world as 'we see it today'. Expecting to be praised for what he himself thinks is a masterpiece, Démogorgon is angered when the other archons mock his creation, and in particular human beings, who have 'so many passions and so little wisdom'. Démogorgon challenges them to make their own worlds, which results in the creation of the other planets of the solar system. The Demiurge declares that all of their creations are imperfect, none of them matching up to the standard of his own work. He expresses the hope that they may do better in the future.

In Voltaire, Gnostic ideas are utilised in the service of Enlightenment philosophy; he himself was not a Gnostic, but found its beliefs a useful tool with which to attack Christianity and the political establishment of his day. A generation after his death saw the first published works of an artist who, while also attacking conventional Christianity and the establishment, actually *was* a Gnostic: William Blake.

Where Blake got his Gnostic beliefs from remains something of a mystery. He lived at a time when Gnostic texts were being recovered from the sands of Egypt, both the Askew and Bruce Codices being discovered during the 1780s and 90s, when Blake was beginning to publish. The critic Crabb Robinson visited Blake and, during a discussion about Wordsworth, Blake expressed his belief that:

'Nature is the work of the devil.' When Robinson pointed out the creation of the earth by God in Genesis, Blake 'repeated the doctrine of the Gnostics with sufficient consistency' that his interviewer was silenced.[198]

Blake's Gnosticism was expressed in the form of a much-misunderstood mythological system, which he elaborated in works such as *The Book of Urizen*, *Vala, or The Four Zoas* and *Jerusalem*. The great Blake scholar Kathleen Raine dismissed the belief that Blake's system was essentially a fiction of his own making:

> People thought – and WB Yeats [who edited an edition of Blake's poems] gave currency to the idea – that Blake made it all up; that he was a mystic... he wasn't. He was a Gnostic... It was gnosis. It wasn't mysticism. He was a Gnostic and he was enormously deeply read.[199]

While Blake's mythology is, like other Gnostic systems, too complex to go into here at length, a brief outline will at least reveal its Gnostic outlook. Originally, the True God beyond being was a divine family of which Christ and the Divine Man (in this case, Albion, not Adam) were members. Within Albion exists four aspects, which are Urizen (Reason), Luvah (Passion), Tharmas (Sensation) and Urthona (Instinct). Albion falls into a passive state and Urizen becomes dominant; only Urthona/Los retains any of Albion's divine nature. Urizen, whom we may take for being Blake's Ialdabaoth, creates the material world, 'a wide world of solid obstruction' that imprisons the divine spirit. Urizen himself, though, is not wholly evil, remaining trapped within his own creation, thinking there is none higher. Human beings are as trapped within the world as its creator.

It is Urizen who is responsible for the repressive laws of Church and state, the one who writes 'Thou Shalt Not' over the door of the Chapel in the Garden of Love; organised religion was anathema for Blake, as was anything that prevents the world from being seen as it really is, what he termed 'the mind-forged manacles'. The antidote to this myopic incarceration was to develop one's imagination and to use it creatively, which would result in the *gnosis* of truly perceiving for the first time. As Blake famously wrote in *The Marriage of Heaven and Hell*, 'When the doors of perception are cleansed, man will see everything as it is, infinite.'

Urizen is ultimately redeemed and reincorporated into the divine family, a redemption which reminds us of Blake's essential optimism, which links him to the more hopeful Gnostic schools of the Valentinians and the Hermeticists:

> In Great Eternity every particular form gives forth or emanates
> Its own peculiar light, and the form is the Divine Vision,
> And the light His garment. This is Jerusalem in every man,
> A tent and tabernacle of mutual forgiveness, male and female clothings.
> And Jerusalem is called Liberty among the children of Albion.

Blake championed that most treasured of Gnostic abilities, the creative imagination, whose presence led to the 'new gospel every day' that had so enraged Irenaeus; for Blake, that gospel was 'everlasting', and it called upon its readers to participate in the building of a new Jerusalem:

> He who despises and mocks a mental gift in another, calling it pride, and selfishness and sin, mocks Jesus, the giver of every mental gift, which always appear to the ignorance-loving hypocrite as sins. But that which is a sin in the sight of cruel man is not so in the sight of our kind God. Let every Christian as much as in him lies, engage himself openly and publicly before all the world in some mental pursuit for the building of Jerusalem. [200]

Blake's great German contemporary Goethe also mocked conventional Christianity and, in his great two-part drama, *Faust*, created a thoroughly Gnostic vision of the fall and redemption of the soul. While earlier versions of the Faust story, notably Marlowe's, end with Faust's eternal damnation and the general upholding of the Christian status quo, in Goethe's version, Faust embarks on a libertine path that might have been the envy of the Carpocratians (had they ever been libertines outside the pages of the Church Fathers' rhetoric). Attempting to keep Faust as entangled in the material world as possible, the devil Mephisto makes Faust lust after the innocent Gretchen. In a chain of misfortune reminiscent of the descents of the female protagonist of the Exegesis on the Soul and Simon Magus's Ennoia/Helen, Gretchen falls pregnant and, chastised as a prostitute, is condemned to death. Faust tries to rescue her, but she will not accept his offer of salvation, which has only been made possible through the wiles of Mephisto.

The second part of Faust sees him a wealthy man. He has forgotten all about his love for Gretchen and, when he dies, it would appear that his soul is destined for Mephisto's eternal keeping. However, Mephisto hadn't reckoned on his plan being scuppered by a host of lovely angels appearing just as he and his henchmen are about to carry Faust off. In a ploy recalling the 12 Angels of Light in the Manichaean creation story, the angels enflame the lust of Mephisto and his devils and are able to rescue Faust's soul and transport it to the realm of light. It transpires that this rescue was the result of Gretchen's intercession, who, after her execution at the end of Part One, has herself reached the world of light through penitence. Faust is saved by the Divine Feminine.

The Existentialists

Elements of Gnosticism can also be found in the works of the Existential philosophers, although they themselves would have probably professed ignorance of Gnosticism. Although the Existential school developed in the mid to late nineteenth century in the works of Søren Kierkegaard and Friedrich Nietzsche, its origins go back to the French philosopher Blaise Pascal (1623–62).

Pascal believed that nature and the universe were indifferent to the fate of man, whom he famously described as a 'thinking reed'.

God, for Pascal, was a *deus abscondidus* who was absent from his creation; believing in such a deity was little more than a way of hedging one's bets: if God didn't exist, then you had nothing to lose by being wrong. Pascal saw nothing in nature to suggest that it had been divinely ordained or ordered. Kierkegaard, too, held that God was absent and utterly inscrutable. The gulf separating man from God is so vast that man is left to his own devices, including creating meaning and value for himself. Nietzsche was even more extreme, in uttering his battle-cry, 'God is dead'. Elaborating on this idea, Nietzsche stated that there was no rational justification for positing the existence of a 'beyond' in which a divinity existed. This vacuum led logically to the loss of value and morality, a nihilistic position that went further than the Gnostics had ever done, in that there was no true God existing sublimely in a distant Pleroma to which the believer would one day return.

If man's relation to God was problematic, so too was his relationship with the world. Like the Gnostics, the Existentialists viewed the world as a place of alienation in which man is cast adrift. In addition, man exists largely unaware of his own potential, rather like the Gnostic concept of the hylics being unaware of the divine spark within them. Jean-Paul Sartre, arguably the most important Existentialist of the twentieth century, described these two modes as 'being-in-itself' and 'being-for-itself'. The former is the condition of nature and animals, while the latter is the desired condition of human beings. People are either unaware of their potential, or relinquish control of their lives and so essentially waste away in something akin to a persistent vegetative state. This idea is explored in Sartre's great 1938 novel *Nausea*, in which the protagonist, Roquentin, undergoes a crisis in a French seaside town, which culminates in his realisation that, in order to live fully, he must adopt the 'being-for-itself' way of living.

Although, as we have noted, no Existentialist ever cited the

Gnostics as an influence, a tentative suggestion could be made for the similarities between the two schools. The German historian and philosopher Oswald Spengler drew attention to the early centuries of our era and the twentieth century, believing that both civilisations were at identical phases of their lifecycles. This would imply that we have more in common with the era of classical Gnosticism than would first appear, and may be one of the reasons that the Gnostic worldview has gained an increasingly wide audience.

Despite these sympathies, however, there are pronounced differences between Existentialism and Gnosticism, perhaps the most significant being the absence in Existentialism of any concept of a true God existing beyond the wasteland of this world; there is no Pleroma, no Light. As the Gnostic scholar and bishop Stephan Hoeller notes, 'Modern and postmodern humanity is hopelessly unredeemed, while the Gnostic is filled with the hope of redemption.'[201]

The Occult Revival

If the links between Gnosticism and Existentialism remain tenuous and ultimately problematic (mainly due to the latter's atheism), there is one movement where the links with Gnosticism were not only conscious, but also greatly more sympathetic: that of the great occult revival of the nineteenth century. At the forefront of this revival was the influential figure of Madame Blavatsky (1831–91), the founder of Theosophy and an avowed Gnostic sympathiser.

Born Helena Petrovna Hahn to a family of Russian nobles living in the Ukraine, she spent her early years travelling widely, even managing to spend two years studying under Buddhist lamas in Tibet during the 1850s. She was said to possess psychic powers and soon gathered a school of devotees around her who would regularly witness HPB's – as she was known by those close to her – ability to materialise lost objects or levitate. Amongst her most important books are *Isis Unveiled* and *The Secret Doctrine*. Despite the profusion of books and schismatic acolytes around her, Blavatsky held throughout her life that compassion is 'the law of laws'.

Although Theosophy was not a conscious attempt at reviving Gnosticism, it had a Gnostic sensibility about it, and Blavatsky's sympathy towards the Gnostics lead to nearly 300 pages of writing on the subject. While attempting to synthesise Hindu and Buddhist doctrines with Western esotericism, science and spiritualism, Theosophy also utilises such Eastern concepts as reincarnation and karma, and derives much of its terminology from Sanskrit. Carl Jung, who was born the year that the Theosophical Society was founded (1875) once remarked that Theosophy was 'Gnosticism in Hindu dress'.[202]

Indeed, Madame Blavatsky possessed an almost uncanny insight into Gnosticism, all the more remarkable for the fact that, like everyone else prior to 1945, she had only a few texts and the biased writings of the Church Fathers to go on. She believed that the universe had been created by inferior spiritual beings and regarded the Jehovah of the Old Testament as Satan. Her optimism distanced her from some of the more austere world-hating Gnostics, making her perhaps closer to the Valentinians and Hermeticists in this respect, but she was nonetheless in thorough agreement with much that was Gnostic. Remarkably, she predicted the re-evaluation of Judas Iscariot, suggesting that she intuited the rediscovery of the Gospel of Judas, which did not happen until nearly a century after her death.

Such was Madame Blavatsky's influence in the world of nineteenth-century alternative spirituality, that she seems to have had connections with almost everyone. Her last secretary, GRS Mead, became a Gnostic devotee himself, translating what scriptures there were available at the time and writing the influential book, *Fragments of a Faith Forgotten* (1900). Other luminaries to be influenced by Blavatsky's Gnosticism were WB Yeats, poet, Blake scholar and sometime member of the Gnostically inclined Order of the Golden Dawn; Aleister Crowley; Dion Fortune; and the Gnostic revivalist Samael Aun Weor.[203]

The Gnostic Jung

If anyone were to claim to be Madame Blavatsky's most important successor, at least in spirit, that would arguably be the great Swiss psychologist, Carl Gustav Jung. Interested in religious affairs from an early age, Jung had developed an interest in Gnosticism as early as 1912, when he wrote to Freud outlining his conviction that the concept of the Gnostic Sophia would soon re-enter Western consciousness through the medium of psychoanalysis. Freud did not share Jung's enthusiasm and the two men parted company not long after. Four years after his letter to Freud, Jung experienced a personal crisis which was to change his life, an experience that was decidedly Gnostic in character.

In 1916, Jung's life was stagnant; he was depressed and frustrated. For days on end, his house was filled with an oppressive atmosphere – which all the family and even visitors were aware of – and there were outbreaks of poltergeist phenomena. At the end of his tether, Jung exclaimed, 'For God's sake, what in the world is this?' He was surprised to hear an immediate response from a chorus of voices: 'We have returned from Jerusalem, where we found not what we sought.' Jung was immediately compelled to start writing and, over the next three evenings, completed a work he entitled *Seven Sermons to the Dead*. Taking the form of a prose poem, Jung attributed the *Seven Sermons* to Basilides; the text announces that they were written in Alexandria, the 'city where east and west meet', the city of *gnosis*, an anti-Jerusalem and anti-Rome.

Jung later declared the work to be a 'youthful indiscretion',[204] declining to publish it in his lifetime, save for a few privately printed copies he gave to friends. He was perhaps wary that the work might arouse hostility, which indeed happened when a copy of the *Sermons* found its way into the hands of the theologian Martin Buber, who accused Jung of being a heretic. Jung may also have borne in mind the fate of Herbert Silberer, who, in 1914, published a book about the relationship between psychology and Western esotericism, alchemy in particular, a subject to which Jung himself would later turn. Silberer showed the book to his mentor, Freud, who dismissed the work utterly. Silberer became depressed and was later excommunicated from Freud's circle altogether. In 1923, he hanged himself.

Despite Jung's misgivings about the work, in private he noted that 'all his creative activity has come from these visions and dreams [the *Sermons*], and that everything he accomplished in later life was already contained in them'.[205] A 1975 Jungian conference supported this view, declaring that the *Seven Sermons* are in fact 'the fount and origin' of Jung's work.[206] Each of the sermons begins with the dead asking Basilides to instruct them about a particular topic, ranging from the nature of the world, to the nature of the true God, church and community, and man himself.

The First Sermon starts with Basilides informing the dead of the existence of the Pleroma, which is both empty and full, nothing and everything, which exists within everyone. The Pleroma contains qualities which we see as pairs of opposites: 'fullness and emptiness, the living and the dead, difference and sameness, light and dark, hot and cold, energy and matter, time and space, good and evil, the beautiful and the ugly, the one and the many'.[207] Because the Pleroma exists within us, we also contain these pairs of opposites. However, the trouble sets in 'when we strive for the good and the beautiful, we forget about our essential being, which is differentiation'.[208] That is to say, when we strive for the good and the beautiful, we are also coming up against the evil and the ugly, because the opposites are inextricably linked; you can't have one without the other. The solution is to 'know ourselves as being apart from the pairs of opposites, then we have attained salvation'.[209] In order to know ourselves, we must learn that the opposites should be allowed to engage freely with each other, which ultimately leads to their resolution, while we ourselves keep our distance from them. This is the essence of what Jung called the process of individuation, which came to be the cornerstone of his psychology.

Although the *Seven Sermons to the Dead* was not published until 1963 – two years after Jung's death – he did acknowledge the influence of Gnosticism on his work during his lifetime.[210] He also pointed out further connections between depth psychology and Gnostic concepts: Ialdabaoth, for instance, could be 'the alienated human ego' unaware of its true source, 'the original wholeness of the unconscious'.[211] It is this unawareness that leads us away from our true selves, thereby denying us the possibility of psychological growth, emotional maturity and happiness.

Gnostic Themes in Literature

Jung's interest in Gnosticism spilled over into literature. Arguably the first 'Gnostic' novel of the twentieth century was Hermann Hesse's *Demian*, published in 1919, shortly after Hesse had begun a period of Jungian analysis. The protagonist, Emil Sinclair, is from a well-to-do background, an environment described as a *scheinwelt*, a play on words meaning both 'world of illusion' as well as 'world of light'. The novel charts Sinclair's progress towards this latter world, frequently accompanied by his mysterious school friend Max Demian. Demian urges Sinclair to break through all normal mores and expand his limited view of reality in order that he might fly up to God, 'whose name is Abraxas'. Hesse later admitted that *Demian* was a fictionalised account of the Jungian process of individuation. Gnostic themes recur in some of Hesse's later work, in particular *Steppenwolf* (1928). Harry Haller, the novel's protagonist, feels himself lost in an alien world and sees 'the whole of human life as a violent and ill-fated abortion of the primal mother, a savage and dismal catastrophe of nature'[212] Struggling with his own nature, which he perceives as not only dualistic but 'a chaos of potentialities and impulses', Haller learns that he has to 'forsake this world and to penetrate to a world beyond time. You know, of course, where this other world lies hidden. Only within yourself lies that other reality.'

Hesse was, of course, not the first writer to utilise Gnostic themes in his work. As we have seen, Gnostic ideas have been identified as far back as Voltaire, Blake and Goethe. All three used Gnostic themes consciously, as have a number of subsequent writers.[213] Perhaps the next important writer to do so after Goethe was Herman Melville, whose masterpiece *Moby Dick* is, in its author's own words, 'a wicked book' and 'a book of secrets'. Although nominally a Unitarian, Melville seems to have been a closet Gnostic. *Moby-Dick* is peppered with Biblical references, including a quote from Genesis at the very beginning, 'And God created great whales', which links the deity with the object of Captain Ahab's quest. It is a deity he campaigns relentlessly against:

> Thou knowest not how came ye, hence callest thyself unbegotten: certainly knowest not thy beginning, hence callest thyself unbegun. I know that of me, which thou knowest not of thyself, oh thou omnipotent. There is some unsuffusing thing beyond thee to whom all thy eternity is but time, all thy creativeness mechanical.[214]

This would be close to blasphemy, were it not for the 'some unsuffusing thing beyond thee' which Ahab can 'dimly see'. Ahab's quest to destroy the whale can be seen as nothing less than a comprehensive revolt against the Demiurge and all his works. The novel's end has a distinctly Gnostic tone, too: Ishmael, the sole survivor from the Pequod (the name means 'orphan') clings to a piece of flotsam in the middle of the ocean, which could be taken to be a metaphor for the Gnostic seeker, Melville himself perhaps, an orphan from the world of light adrift in a material and brutal creation.

Gnostic themes have also been detected in the work of Franz Kafka. Although Jewish by birth, Kafka seems to have been something of an atheist whose sympathy towards religious ideas was, it has been argued, 'morally and existentially motivated'.[215] He had books about Gnosticism on his shelves and belonged to a group of self-styled 'New Marcionites' who dominated the Prague literary scene of the time. Kafka, perhaps aware of Gnosticism's probably Jewish origins, was also interested in trends within Judaism around the same time that Gnosticism was beginning to flourish. His thinking was dominated by a dualism that saw man as being bound both to earth and to heaven; earth could never be left behind, heaven never entered. Earthly life was a prison and it is only at death that one starts to attain knowledge. The 'first sign of beginning knowledge', he wrote in one of his notebooks, 'is the wish to die'.[216] Although the better world seems to be unattainable, Kafka believed that 'there is nothing but a spiritual world; what we call the sensory world is the evil in the spiritual one'.[217] If all of life occurs within this spiritual sphere, ethics and morality take on prime significance, as they are the means by which one can attain the spiritual world. (Art, for Kafka, was also another means.)

Gnostic ideas were not consigned solely to Kafka's notebooks and journals. In *The Castle*, the object of the protagonist's quest is to gain admittance to the castle in order to carry out some surveying work for the count. His failure to do so has been interpreted as showing the total lack of contact between human beings and the divine, depicting reality as both hostile and evil. It is man's task to shatter this reality and to attain the world of light.[218] In *The Trial*, the Gnostic view of the human situation is encapsulated in the parable of the Law and the Doorkeeper. The Law, to which all men strive, represents the true God, whose light can be seen as 'the radiance that streams inextinguishably from the door of the Law.' A doorkeeper, however, guards the door of the Law, allowing no one access. In doing so, he fulfils the role of an archon, in thwarting man's attempts to reach God. The moral of Kafka's parable seems to be that, if man is to return to his true home in the world of light, he must see through the doorkeepers and other powers of this world, and use all his resources to outwit them.

The fields of fantasy and science fiction have proved a fertile ground for gnostically inclined writers. Contemporary with Kafka was the Anglo-Scottish author David Lindsay, who has a fair claim to being fantasy literature's first great Gnostic of the twentieth century. His masterpiece, *A Voyage to Arcturus* (1920), is effectively a Gnostic *Pilgrim's Progress*, although Gnostic ideas run through almost all of his subsequent work as well. As his biographer, Bernard Sellin, comments:

> Any list of the analogies between Lindsay's ideology and the Gnostic cults would be a long one... it would be necessary to cite the importance attached to spirit, the systematic depreciation of the body and the flesh, man as a stranger in the world, the conception of an evil world, indeed an evil God, the cult of the Mother and the Eternal Female, and the condemnation of sexuality.[219]

A Voyage to Arcturus recounts a journey by two men, Maskull and Nightspore, to the planet Tormance, which orbits the binary star Arcturus, whose deity is an entity known variously as Crystalman, Shaping or Surtur. Maskull learns that Krag, the man who has taken them to this strange new world, is said to be Crystalman's nemesis, effectively Tormance's devil. As the story progresses, however, it becomes clear that Crystalman is not all he seems, and neither is Krag.

Maskull wakes on a plain of red sand, naked, to find that his two fellow-travellers are nowhere in sight. He has also developed new sensory organs, including a tentacle that protrudes from his heart. The new world he is on is full of strange colours and life forms, and Tormance's gravity means that he is not able to stand, only kneel. A beautiful young woman called Joiwind appears, offering him both clothing and the means by which he can withstand the planet's gravitational pull: a blood transfusion. She explains that the new organ he has developed on his forehead allows him to read other people's thoughts, while the tentacle enables him to love others. Maskull claims to be affected by a strange light in the sky; Joiwind explains that this is the light from Tormance's second sun, Alppain, which can only be seen by heading north. Wanting to see this light, Maskull soon embarks on a quest that takes him through Tormance's wildly differing landscapes, from the Ifdawn Marest – a mountainous region subject to frequent and hugely violent earthquakes – to the broad valley of Matterplay, whose rivers contain a suffocating preponderance of life forms, many of which are generated spontaneously from out of thin air.

Maskull comes to realise that there is more to his quest to see Alppain's light than he initially believed. He soon encounters Surtur himself, who informs Maskull that Tormance is his world and that Maskull must serve him. Surtur's image enlarges to fill the sky before suddenly vanishing. Maskull encounters further characters in his quest and it becomes clear that many of them represent different ways of life and belief. Joiwind and her husband Panawe are lovers of their world, enthralled by its many pleasures but also aware of its dangers. Oceaxe is a strong, domineering woman whose willpower governs her life, while Sullenbode is sensual, 'a mass of pure sex'. The male characters, too, all seem to be driven by one main outlook. The ascetic Spadevil lives life according to a sense of duty, while Corpang and the androgynous – for want of a better word – Leehallfae are intensely religious, but deluded. Only the Zen-like fisherman, Polecrab, seems to be content and it is with him that Maskull has one of the most significant conversations in the book:

> 'Since I've come out of that forest,' proceeded Maskull, talking to himself, 'a change has come over me, and I see things differently. Everything here looks much more solid and real in my eyes than in other places... so much so that I can't entertain the least doubt of its existence. It not only *looks* real, it is real – and on that I would stake my life... But at the same time that it's real, it is *false*.'
> 'Like a dream?'
> 'No – not at all like a dream, and that's just what I want to explain. This world of yours – and perhaps mine too, for that matter – doesn't give me the slightest impression of a dream, or an illusion, or anything of that sort. I know it's really here at this moment, and it's exactly as we're seeing it, you and I. Yet it's false. It's false in this sense, Polecrab. Side by side with it another world exists, and that other world is the true one, and this one is all false and deceitful, to the very core. And so it occurs to me that reality and falseness are two words for the same thing.'[220]

The concept of two worlds, a higher and a lower, recur throughout the book. In Matterplay, Maskull has a vision in which he can see green sparks flying upwards from the brook:

> Each one wavering up towards the clouds, but the moment they got within them, a fearful struggle seemed to begin. The spark endeavoured to escape through to the upper air, while the clouds concentrated around it, whichever way it darted, trying to create so dense a prison around it, that further movement would be impossible.[221]

Although most of the sparks escape, some don't and sink slowly towards the ground again, where they become denser and darker, ultimately becoming matter (in this case a strange walking plant–animal hybrid). The escaping sparks of Matterplay are counterbalanced by Nightspore's vision in the stone tower on the island of Muspel, which represents Tormance's sole bastion of the higher world – what Lindsay termed the Sublime. He looks out of the window to see Crystalman living off the energies (the green sparks are visible again) of all Tormance's inhabitants. The lower, vulgar world is literally leeching its denizens to death.

The cold fury of this final vision was not something Lindsay adopted for this one book. As we have noted, Gnostic themes were to recur in all his subsequent work,[222] which, in varying ways, show that 'reality is the progress homeward of the fragments of spirit',[223] but perhaps never so forcefully as in this mind-bending first novel. 'The Sublime is not a metaphysical theory,' Lindsay later wrote, 'but a terrible fact which stands above and behind the world and governs all its manifestations.'[224]

Since Lindsay, arguably no writer has employed Gnosticism more consciously than Philip K Dick, whose fiction abounds with false realities and salvific knowledge, often appearing in the world in the unlikely guise of graffiti in a men's room, or in the apparently random arrangement of rubbish in an alleyway.[225] Dick had a lifelong interest in philosophical and theological questions, and seems to have become interested in Gnosticism in the mid 1960s. However, he did not consciously begin to employ Gnostic themes in his fiction until after experiencing a series of mystical life-changing events in early 1974. His autobiographical 1981 novel *VALIS* – an acronym for Vast Active Living Intelligence System – describes the events of 1974 and the struggles of his hero, Horselover Fat, to keep hold of what sanity he has left. Fat – his name is a multilingual version of Dick's own, Philip meaning 'lover of horses' in Greek and

Dick being 'fat' in German – experiences a theophany when a mysterious beam of pink light is fired into his head. His grip on reality, tenuous at the best of times, slips even further as Fat develops his own concepts about God. In one memorable scene, he attempts to explain the Gnostic creation myth to his psychiatrist, the long-suffering Maurice:

> 'Do you believe man is created in God's image?' Maurice said.
> 'Yes', Fat said, '[...] but the creator deity, not the true God.'
> 'What?' Maurice said.
> 'That's Ialdabaoth. Sometimes called Samael, the blind god. He's deranged.'
> 'What the hell are you talking about?' Maurice said. [...] 'Who made this stuff up? You?'
> 'Basically', Fat said, 'my doctrine is Valentinian, second century CE.'[26]

Maurice, a staunch believer in the Bible, is so incensed by Fat's Gnostic beliefs that he gives Fat homework: to read the Book of Genesis twice and copy out the main ideas and events it contains. Fat leaves the session, realising that 'bringing up the topic of God had been a poor idea'. *VALIS* is, amongst other things, a comic *tour de force*.

Fat's Gnostic beliefs recur throughout the novel in the form of his journal, or *Tractate: Cryptica Scriptura* as he calls it, thinking that the Latin sounds better than the English title of 'hidden discourse'. In this, Fat sketches out a 'two source cosmogony', which posits 'One mind' but under which 'two principles contend': these are the principles of illusion and reality, the world of illusion (the everyday world) and the world of *gnosis* (the real world beyond Ialdabaoth's control). Original sin is likewise dealt with in the most Gnostic of fashions in entry 29 of Fat's *Tractate*:

We did not fall because of moral error; we fell because of an intellectual error: that of taking the phenomenal world as real. Therefore we are morally innocent. It is the [Roman] Empire in its various disguised polyforms which tells us we have sinned. 'The Empire never ended.'[227]

Fat's system also holds that the illusory world of everyday reality is 'still secretly ruled by the hidden race descended from Ikhnaton', which is his way of expressing the Valentinian belief that Sophia and her aeons have managed to penetrate the Demiurge's creation in order to bring gnosis to those who are able to receive it.

This idea of salvific knowledge penetrating the mundane world is one of Dick's most recurrent Gnostic themes, occurring in such novels as *Ubik*, *Radio Free Albemuth* and *Galactic Pot Healer*. The theme of the world as both illusion and prison recurs in *Ubik*, again (arguably Dick's masterpiece), *Eye in the Sky*, *A Maze of Death* and *Flow My Tears, the Policeman Said*. In *The Simulacra*, the fake nature of Western civilisation is brilliantly encapsulated in the figure of the President of the United States, who is found to be an android, and also in the form of commercials that are miniaturised robotic insects that can bite people with all the effectiveness of a malarial mosquito. In *Do Androids Dream of Electric Sheep?* (the novel on which Ridley Scott's film *Blade Runner* was based), the distractions of modern life — such as junk mail, TV, door-to-door salesmen, shopping malls — are all designated as 'kipple', a neologism coined by Dick that effectively means 'shit'. Despite — or perhaps even because of — the difficulties of discerning the real from the fake and the android from the human, Dick's work is ultimately optimistic, or as Horselover Fat put it, 'my doctrine is Valentinian, second century CE'. *VALIS* concludes hopefully with a final entry from Fat's *Tractate*, a thoroughly Gnostic comment that reminds us that, once we have *gnosis*, we are the same as Moses, Elijah and Christ himself:

From Ikhnaton this knowledge [gnosis] passed to Moses, and from Moses to Elijah, the Immortal Man, who became Christ. But underneath all the names there is only one Immortal Man; and we are that man.[228]

Gnosticism in Popular Culture

Philip K Dick is arguably one of the most important writers of the late twentieth and early twenty-first centuries, in that he predicted a media and technology-obsessed culture, but paradoxically a culture that also longs – at least in part – for transcendence and the knowledge that there is in fact still a world to transcend to. His Gnostic vision seems to have influenced a wide variety of comics, computer games and movies. Neil Gaiman's *Sandman* series, for instance, is broadly Gnostic in cosmological structure, while Alan Moore exhibits pronounced Gnostic tendencies in *The Watchmen*. Moore evokes the concept of Voegelin's 'immanentisation of the eschaton' in the shape of Adrian Veidt / Ozymandias' plot to save the world by tricking people into believing that an alien invasion is imminent. Moore's graphic novel *Promethea* explores Gnostic issues even more directly, through the vehicle of Kabbalistic, alchemical and other esoteric framing devices.

The *Final Fantasy* and *Xenosaga* series of computer role-playing games likewise allude to Gnostic myth in varying degrees, as does *Dungeons & Dragons*. Tori Amos's 2005 album *The Beekeeper* contains three songs which reflect her Gnostic interests, 'Original Sinsuality', 'Marys of the Sea' and 'The Beekeeper'. She also explores Gnosticism in her autobiography, *Piece By Piece*. In the realms of television, Gnosticism has appeared to varying degrees in episodes of *Doctor Who* ('The Parting of the Ways') and *Stargate SG1* (the ninth series in particular). Peter Weir's film *The Truman Show* bears a strong resemblance to Philip K Dick's 1959 novel *Time Out of Joint*. In the film, Jim Carrey's character becomes obsessed with the idea that the world in which he lives is totally fake. His instinct is right: his world has been created by a television company for a reality TV show. (We could infer that the need for ratings could be another of Ialdabaoth's archonic tricks.)

Gnosticism, though, has perhaps been best represented in popular culture by the Wachowski brothers' film *The Matrix*, which, again, seems to owe its world view at least in part to Philip K Dick and, by extension, to the Gnostics. The film tells the story of a computer hacker known as Neo (Keanu Reeves), who comes into the knowledge that the world is in fact a giant computer simulation, designed to keep human beings in a state of slavery to the machines which designed it. We later learn that these machines were originally given artificial intelligence by humans, but then rebelled against their creators, imprisoning them and feeding off their energy.

Although the film contains elements drawn from mainstream Christian tradition – Neo is referred to repeatedly as 'the One' (a redeemer figure long prophesied), the rebels' ship is called the *Nebuchadnezzar* and their stronghold is Zion – the film seems to draw more on Gnostic sources. Indeed, near the beginning of the film, Neo falls asleep in front of his computer. He is woken by a mysterious message that appears on the screen, which reads 'Wake up, Neo.' This is essentially the theme of the film, and needless to say, it is Gnostic. Trinity (Carrie-Anne Moss) and Morpheus (Laurence Fishburne) are, as they instruct and aid Neo in waking up, playing aeonic roles as opposed to the archonic Agent Smith (Hugo Weaving), who attempts to keep Neo inside the Matrix and therefore asleep to ultimate reality. The film employs terms that are also found in Gnostic texts, such as blindness, sleep, ignorance, dreaming, darkness and night which stand in opposition to seeing, waking, knowing and light. It is these latter states to which Neo travels and ultimately attains.[229]

The First Christian Heretics

That Gnosticism enjoys more popularity today than at any other time in its history owes a lot, ironically, to the imperialistic literalist Christian culture that helped extirpate it in the first place. Europe's expansion into Africa and Asia during the eighteenth century facilitated the archaeological digs that resulted in the discovery of the Askew, Bruce and Berlin Codices. This in turn led, indirectly, to the foundation of new Gnostic churches, especially in France and latterly in the United States, where they still exist today. The increasingly tolerant West of today is of course also a factor in allowing people of Gnostic inclinations to practise their faith again openly for the first time in nearly 2,000 years. But one is forced to wonder, have the Gnostics come back to us today for a reason?

It is interesting to recall the words of the Gospel of the Egyptians, which speaks of the burial of the Gnostic scriptures 'in the mountain that is called Charaxio' where they will lie until 'the end of the times and the eras', when they will be unearthed and reveal 'love, and the great, invisible eternal Spirit, and his only begotten Son, and the eternal light... and the incorruptible Sophia... and the whole Pleroma in eternity'. It is interesting to note that the Nag Hammadi scriptures were discovered in what is arguably the worst year in human history, 1945. On 27 January that year, Allied forces liberated, and discovered the true horror of, Auschwitz-Birkenau; on 15 April, the ghastly realities of Bergen-Belsen likewise came to light; on 16 July, the nuclear age began with the first Trinity test in New Mexico; on 6 August, Hiroshima was vaporised by the first atomic bomb, 'Little Boy'. Three days later, its brother, 'Fat Man', did the same for Nagasaki. Is it merely wishful thinking that Gnostic wisdom has come back to us at precisely the time when humanity seems to need it most? That is ultimately for each of us to decide.

After the horrific events of 9/11, we are living in a world which is seemingly governed by nothing other than corporate greed and fundamentalist religion – Christian, Muslim and Jewish. Politicians and religious leaders from all sides want to score points – and take lives – by insisting on the literal truth of their own faith. The Gnostics, never ones for martyrdom, stand in eternal opposition to the high and the mighty of this world. They know that it is a world which can be transcended, but, in doing so, it is also necessary to 'love your brother as your soul; keep him as the apple of your eye';[230] Gnosticism, while being practical, is also compassionate and understands the tendency of the human mind to create divisions where there are none.

And finally it must be remembered that, far from being the 'first Christian heretics', the Gnostics were almost certainly closer to Jesus's original teachings than the official Church ever was. If anyone can be called the 'first Christian heretics', it is without a doubt the bishops who sat at the Council of Nicaea in 325. In attempting to create orthodoxy, they instead created a monster which controlled people's minds and lives for nearly 2,000 years. Again, one wonders whether the discovery at Nag Hammadi was not only timely, but necessary, a feeling borne out by the Jungian analyst Murray Stein, who wrote that we are living in a culture that:

> ...cannot accept difference without polarizing it and that attempts only to reform, convert, or eliminate those who differ. This is precisely the attitude imaged as Ialdabaoth by the Gnostics two thousand years ago.[231]

This seems to be exactly the mindset that has created trouble in the Middle East – and Iraq in particular – and that also, according to the more conspiratorially inclined, is the mindset that will drive the President of the United States to initiate, in conjunction with Israel, Armageddon in order to fulfil Biblical prophecy. Gnostics would scoff at such a notion, were the threat not so real. Stein again:

Ialdabaoth represents the ground plan of the individualistic, controlling, narcissistic ego so familiar in Western culture. What the Gnostics identified and named in Ialdabaoth is still with us, perhaps even more so.[232]

But it would be wrong, perhaps, to finish our survey of Gnosticism on such a dark note. We know not when the hour cometh, as Horselover Fat discovered in *VALIS*, the end of which sees him sitting at home, in one of Philip K Dick's most moving scenes, waiting for the Second Coming to appear on television. If it happens at all, however, it will not appear on TV: it will happen within ourselves, and will be, as the Treatise on the Resurrection puts it, a life- and heart-changing new knowledge of 'the truth which stands firm. It is the revelation of what is, and the transformation of things, and a transition into newness'.[233]

This, it would seem, is the wisdom the world needs, not that of dogmatic, hate-filled orthodox religion. The fount of this wisdom is not to be found coming from the mouths of priests, rabbis and mullahs – who may lead us astray, into violence, narrow-mindedness and hatred – but within ourselves. Gnosticism may deny that this world is our true home, but it never fails to remind us that the source of liberation lies within us all:

Light the lamp within you... Knock on yourself as upon a door and walk upon yourself as on a straight road. For if you walk on the road, it is impossible for you to go astray.[234]

Appendix I: Glossary

Abraxas   A redeemed archon who came to occupy the seventh heaven. He is often depicted on Gnostic amulets and gems. For Jung, he was the very essence of Gnosticism

aeon   An emanated aspect of the divine, often represented as being male/female pairs

Apocryphon   A Greek word meaning 'secret book'. The most well-known Apocryphon is that of John, but there are also Apocryphons of James and Mark

archon   A ruler of the celestial spheres of the material world, they are amongst the chief obstacles on the road to completing the spiritual journey

barbarous words   Words not originating from any known language, usually consisting of long strings of vowels, used in Gnostic rituals and inscribed on Gnostic amulets

Barbelo   The divine feminine, God the Mother

Deficiency   The material world

Demiurge   The creator of the material world. Often identified with the God of the Old Testament, he is usually seen as arrogant, incompetent and even sometimes as evil

emanation   According to the Gnostics, all things are, originally, emanations from the divine. It is the Demiurge who gives them physical properties

Ennoia   Another name for Barbelo, the divine female principle

eschaton, immanentising the   Coined by the political philosopher Eric Voegelin, the phrase refers to the attempt to bring what is expected in the afterlife to pass in this life, creating heaven on earth. Voegelin accused the Gnostics of essentially attempting to bring on the end of the world

gnosis   Intuitive, direct knowledge of the divine. Gnostics held that *gnosis* alone was the key to salvation

gospel   Good news. In Gnostic terms, this refers to any text whose aim is to advance the Gnostic message. All Gnostic gospels were deemed heretical by the Church. Amongst the most well known are the Gospels of Thomas, Mary and Philip

Hebdomad   The ninth sphere of the cosmos, usually seen as the lowest part of the Pleroma

hylics   One of the three main classes of people, according to the Valentinians. Hylics are resolutely 'in matter' and are concerned solely with the concerns of the flesh. Compare *psychics* and *pneumatics*

Ialdabaoth   The name of the Demiurge, usually taken to mean 'childish god'

Logion   A saying, usually of Jesus. The Gospel of Thomas is an example of a gospel made up entirely of logia, with little or no narrative

logos   The word of God which, in Gnostic texts, can also refer to Jesus as well

manda   Gnosis, in the Mandaean tongue

mandaiia   Mandaean believers

nasuraiia   Mandaean priests

Ogdoad   The eight spheres of the material cosmos, above which lay the ninth, the heavenly Hebdomad

Pistis   Faith

Pleroma   The fullness, the heavenly realm beyond material creation

pneumatics   The pneumatics are spiritually aware people, who are above dogma and division, and who are able to receive *gnosis*

psychics   The psychics are people who are not so caught up in the pleasures and pains of earthly existence, but who are more inclined to thinking, feeling and participating in exoteric (i.e., dogmatic) religion

Saklas   Another name for the Demiurge, meaning 'fool'

Samael   Another name for the Demiurge, meaning 'blind god'

Serpent   In Gnostic creation myths, the Serpent is the wise teacher who is responsible for Eve attaining *gnosis* by eating the fruit of the Tree of Knowledge. She then instructs Adam to do the same. In some variations of the myth, it is Christ himself who plays the role of the Serpent

Sophia   The youngest emanation. Her desire to know the father leads to the creation of Ialdabaoth, who in turn creates the material world. Some versions of the story have two Sophias, a higher and a lower. The higher Sophia remains in the Pleroma, while the lower Sophia remains trapped in matter

Appendix II: Gnosticism and Buddhism

The Buddhist scholar Edward Conze has noted certain similarities between Gnosticism and Buddhism. The main similarities are:

1. Salvation takes place through *gnosis* or knowledge. Conversely, ignorance leads to one remaining trapped in the material world.
2. A tendency towards elitism, such as the Elect and Listeners of Manichaeism and the Rinpoches and Lamas of Buddhism.
3. Wisdom appears in the two faiths as both a virtue and as an aspect of the deity.
4. Both Gnostics and Buddhists favour myths over facts.
5. There is an antinomian tendency in both.
6. Both differentiate between the stillness of the true God/Nirvana and the active creator God, who exists on a lower level. The world is the abode of evil archons, while in Buddhism it is ruled over by Mara, the evil deity.
7. Both traditions favour esotericism, resisting easy popularity.
8. Both traditions have a monistic metaphysics, in which reunification with the one is to be sought at the expense of rejecting the many (i.e., the material world).

In addition, both traditions have been seen as somewhat pessimistic and anything from world-denying to outright world-hating. Both are pacifist religions and both have suffered persecution.

Whether Buddhism and Gnosticism directly influenced one another remains uncertain, but as there were Buddhist missionaries in Alexandria in the first and second centuries CE, an interplay between the two faiths remains a distinct possibility.

Appendix III: Gnosticism in the Canonical Gospels

Be still and know — Psalm 46

As has been noted, some scholars now believe that the Gospel of Thomas could be one of the oldest of all surviving gospels — Gnostic or otherwise — which suggests Gnosticism has a fair claim to being one of the original forms of Christianity before the Church Fathers stamped it out. However, in their desire to establish a decidedly non-Gnostic canon, they seem to have overlooked some curious moments in the canonical gospels, where it seems that there were two sides to Jesus's teachings, where concepts central to Gnosticism, such as secrecy, knowing, death and spiritual rebirth, are present. That is not to suggest that Jesus was a Gnostic, but Matthew 13.10–17 shows that there was an esoteric side to what he taught:

> And the disciples came and said to him: Why speakest thou to them in parables? He answered and said unto them: it is given unto you to *know* [author's italics] the secrets of the kingdom of heaven, but to them, it is not given...Therefore I speak to them in similitudes [parables]: for though they see, they see not: and hearing, they hear not: neither understand.[235]

The same section also contains two sentences that are highly reminiscent of the Gospel of Thomas (logion 41):

> For whosoever hath to him shall be given: and he shall have abundance. But whosoever hath not: from him shall be taken away even that [what] he hath.[236]

The Gospels of Mark and Luke also contain variations on the discussion about the use of parables,[237] with Mark adding the additional phrase that parables are for 'them that are without',[238] which could be interpreted as 'those who are not on the spiritual path'; or, maybe, those who have not experienced *gnosis*.

Two further examples to ponder: in Matthew, Chapter 6, we find Jesus exhorting the disciples how to pray:

> But when thou prayest, enter into thy chamber, and shut thy door to thee, and pray to thy father which is *in secret* [author's italics]: and thy father which seeth in secret, shall reward thee openly.[239]

And then there is the mysterious utterance by Thomas the Twin in John Chapter 11, when Jesus informs the disciples that Lazarus is dead: 'let us also go,' says Thomas, 'that we may die with him'.[240] Ruling out some kind of suicide pact, as we must, this could be interpreted as a metaphorical death – an initiation ceremony, perhaps? A similar scene occurs in the Gnostic Secret Gospel of Mark, where Jesus raises a young man from the tomb. Afterwards, the young man 'spent that night with him [Jesus], because Jesus taught him the mystery of God's domain'.[241]

Endnotes

Epigraph: Recognitions II.37, Quoted in Rudolph, p.297.

1. The Gospel of Thomas, Prologue and Saying 1 from *The Nag Hammadi Library in English*, p.126.

2. The Gospel of Thomas, from *The Apocryphal New Testament*, p.140.

3. Matthew 5.15: 'No one lights a lamp and puts it under a bowl; instead he puts it on the lampstand, where it gives light for everyone in the house.' (Good News Bible translation.)

4. Mark 4.34, Good News Bible translation. Also Mark 4.10–11, which suggests that the teachings the disciples were given when they were alone with Jesus was not what Jesus preached in public.

5. e.g. Matthew 12,46–50; Mark 3.31 35; Luke 8.19–21; Thomas echoes this in Saying 99.

6. John 11.16, 20.24 and 21.2.

7. Saying 29, *Nag Hammadi Library in English*, p.130.

8. The Gospel of Thomas, Saying 70, *The Complete Gospels*, p.316.

9. Justin Martyr, *Apology* II, cited in Pagels, *The Gnostic Gospels*, p.100.

10. Acts of Peter 31. *The Apocryphal New Testament*, p.422.

11. Stephan Hoeller, *Gnosticism: New Light on the Ancient Tradition of Inner Knowing*, p.3.

12. Irenaeus, *Against the Heretics*, cited in Pagels, p.17.

13. Hippolytus, *Refutation of All Heresies*, Pagels, p.17. Hippolytus also condemned Jews and Pagans.

14. Tertullian, *De Carne Christi*, quoted in Pagels, p.36.

15. Matthew 16.18: 'And so I tell you, Peter: you are a rock, and on this rock foundation I will build my church.'

16. See, for instance, Robert Eisenman's *James the Brother of Jesus* (Faber and Faber, 1997).

17. 1 Corinthians 11:24–25, when Paul quotes from Jesus's words at the Last Supper. In 2 Corinthians 12:9, Paul claims that Jesus spoke to him

directly, saying 'My grace is all you need, for my power is strongest when you are weak.' If this is indeed a genuine quote, then 2 Corinthians would seem to have a world exclusive on this phrase as it appears nowhere else in the New Testament.

18. AN Wilson, *Paul: The Mind of the Apostle*, p.258.

19. Michael Baigent and Richard Leigh in *The Dead Sea Scrolls Deception*, p.266.

20. Thomas Jefferson, from a letter to W Short published in *The Great Thoughts* by George Sildes (Ballantine Books, 1985), p.208.

21. Some scholars believe that the Gospel of Thomas is as old as the four canonicals, making it the oldest of the Gnostic gospels and, perhaps, the most authentic in that it may actually contain Jesus's genuine words.

22. Elaine Pagels, *Beyond Belief*, p.150.

23. They were, to quote *Monty Python and the Holy Grail*, 'an anarcho-syndicalist commune taking it in turns to be a sort of executive officer for the week'. Gnostic tendencies have also been detected in *Life of Brian*. John Cleese's immortal line, 'How shall we fuck off, O Lord?' being perhaps the best – and funniest – send-up of literalist religion ever uttered.

24. Quoted in Pagels, *op. cit.*, pp.60–61.

25. Kurt Rudolph, *Gnosis*, p.278.

26. Rudolph p.281, quoting Wisdom of Solomon 6, 18f; 8, 17.

27. Rudolph p.281, further quotes following.

28. Rudolph, p.282.

29. Mary Boyce, *Zoroastrians: Their Religious Beliefs and Practices* (Routledge and Kegan Paul, 1979), p.1.

30. Boyce, p.29.

31. Another development during the Achaemenid era was an offshoot of Zoroastrianism, Zurvanism, which held that both Ohrmazd and Ahriman were the twin offspring of the god of time and destiny, Zurvan.

32. Rudolph, p.284. Rudolph also notes the Hellenistic influence on the Old Testament: 'the scepticism of Ecclesiastes cannot be fully understood without the Greek rationalism and the early Hellenistic popular philosophy'.

33. Stuart Holroyd, *The Elements of Gnosticism*, p.9.

34. The Gospel of Truth, *The Nag Hammadi Library in English*, p.42.

35. Excerpta de Theodoto, quoted in Hoeller, *op. cit.*, p.10.

36. The Gospel of Philip, *The Nag Hammadi Library in English*, p.159.

37. Hoeller, *op. cit.*, pp.5–6.
38. Yuri Stoyanov, *The Other God*, p.2. The leading Orientalist of his time, Hyde (1636–1703) was chief librarian at the Bodleian Library in Oxford; he coined the word 'cuneiform' and investigated the origins of chess.
39. Ugo Bianchi, *Il dualismo religioso* (Rome, 1958), quoted in Stoyanov, *ibid.*, pp.4–5.
40. On the Origin of the World, *The Nag Hammadi Library in English*, p.173.
41. The Gospel of Philip, *The Gnostic Bible*, p.277.
42. The Testimony of Truth, *The Nag Hammadi Library in English*, p.455.
43. Luke 23.34.
44. Preserved by Hippolytus in his *Philosophumena*.
45. Irenaeus, *Against Heresies*, quoted in Pagels, *Beyond Belief*, p.80.
46. For instance, all prophecies of Christ's coming are removed, as is the concept that he is the Jewish messiah.
47. Or, rather, what Marcion regarded as the core of the Pauline corpus: Galatians, Corinthians, Romans, Thessalonians, Ephesians, Colossians, Philippians and Philemon.
48. GRS Mead, *Fragments of a Faith Forgotten* 2, quoted in Hoeller, *op. cit.*, p.113.
49. The exact dates for Pius I's papacy have not been established. He may have reigned from 140 to 154, though the Vatican's 2003 *Annuario Pontificio* lists 142 or 146 to 157 or 161.
50. Hoeller, *op. cit.*, pp.100–1.
51. It is quite possible that the Templars' supposed heresy – assuming they had any at all – was Gnosticism. They could have become exposed to Gnosticism through contact in the East with either Sufi groups, and/or Mandaean groups.
52. Mount Seir does actually get mentioned a number of times in the Old Testament, but never in relation to the Flood.
53. Hoeller, *op. cit.*, p.101. He then quotes Jacques Lacarierre's observation that 'one can pursue the Gnostics, but one cannot seize hold of them'.
54. Tertullian, quoted in Rudolph, p.215.
55. The Gospel of Philip, *The Nag Hammadi Library in English*, p.150. There may have actually been seven sacraments, thus mirroring the seven sacraments of the mainstream Church.
56. Hoeller, *op. cit.*, p.85.
57. For a fuller discussion, see Lupieri, pp.8–10.

58. There is further speculation that *nasuraiia* derives from 'Nasorean' or 'Nazarene', suggesting a connection with these groups. See Lupieri, pp.9–10.

59. *The Gnostic Bible*, p.537.

60. *The Gnostic Bible*, p.542.

61. *The Gnostic Bible*, p.549.

62. *The Gnostic Bible*, p.550.

63. *The Gnostic Bible*, pp.550–1.

64. 'Nazareth' may well be a mistranslation of 'Nasorean' or 'Nazarene', both of whom were fringe Jewish groups to whom Jesus was thought to have possibly belonged at one time. Nazareth, as a town, almost certainly did not exist in the early decades of the first century CE, precisely the time that Jesus was supposed to have lived there.

65. *The Gnostic Bible*, p.601.

66. Manichaean psalms, quoted in Hoeller, *op. cit.*, p.138.

67. Manichaean psalm, quoted in Hoeller, *op. cit.*, p.138.

68. The Coptic Manichaean Songbook 12, *The Gnostic Bible*, p.622.

69. Asclepius, *The Nag Hammadi Library in English*, p.333.

70. Asclepius, *The Nag Hammadi Library in English*, p.335.

71. The Discourse on the Eighth and Ninth, *The Nag Hammadi Library in English*, p.322.

72. The Discourse on the Eighth and Ninth, *The Nag Hammadi Library in English*, p.325.

73. The Discourse on the Eighth and Ninth, *The Nag Hammadi Library in English*, p.326.

74. Poimandres, *The Gnostic Bible*, p.509.

75. Corpus Hermeticum, Libellus XIII, *Hermetica*, p.99.

76. See, for instance, Joseph Dan's *Kabbalah: A Very Short Introduction*, which denies any links to Gnosticism.

77. Marvin Meyer, Introduction to Islamic Mystical Literature, *The Gnostic Bible*, p.663.

78. Abd' al-Khâliq Ghijduwâni, *Travelling the Path of Love*, p.16.

79. This incident forms the basis of Agraphon, a poem by the Greek poet Angelos Sikelianos (1884–1951). The title means 'unwritten [i.e., apocryphal] thing'. It has been set to music by Sir John Tavener, and appears on the *Total Eclipse* CD (Harmonia Mundi HMU 907271).

80. *The Gnostic Bible*, pp.660–2.

81. The Mother of Books, *The Gnostic Bible*, p.725.

82. Kreyenbroek, Philip G, *Yezidism – Its Background, Observances and Textual*

Tradition, p.2, quoting the French explorer FB Charmoy, who published his findings about the Yezidis in 1868.

83. The Apocryphon of John, *The Gnostic Bible*, p.138.
84. The Apocryphon of John, *The Gnostic Bible*, p.139.
85. The Apocryphon of John, *The Gnostic Bible*, pp.139–140.
86. The Apocryphon of John, *The Gnostic Bible*, p.141.
87. The Apocryphon of John, *The Gnostic Bible*, p.146.
88. The Apocryphon of John, *The Gnostic Bible*, p.147.
89. The Apocryphon of John, *The Gnostic Bible*, p.149.
90. The Apocryphon of John, *The Gnostic Bible*, p.162.
91. The Apocryphon of John, *The Gnostic Bible*, p.164.
92. The Gospel of Truth, *The Gnostic Bible*, p.249.
93. The Greek fragments were Oxy 1, 654 & 655, containing sayings 26–30, 77 and 31–33. For a parallel text edition of the Coptic and Greek Thomas, see JK Elliot, pp.123–47.
94. The Gospel of Thomas, *The Apocryphal New Testament*, p.135. What is slightly confusing in most translations is that *didymos* and *Thomas* both mean 'twin', therefore 'Didymus Judas Thomas' means 'The Twin Judas the Twin'.
95. The belief that Christ had a twin brother was deemed heretical. For a fascinating study of the legend and its treatment by artists such as Leonardo, See David Ovason, *The Two Children* (Random House, 2001).
96. The Gospel of Thomas, Logion 2, *Nag Hammadi Library in English*, p.126.
97. The Gospel of Thomas, Logion 70, *The Complete Gospels*, p.316.
98. The Gospel of Thomas, Logion 6, *Nag Hammadi Library in English*, p.127.
99. For an exhaustive list of parallels between the Gospel of Thomas and the canonical gospels, see Elliot, pp. 133–5.
100. Matthew 10:27, Luke 12:3, Mark 4:21, Luke 8:16, 11:33, Matthew 5:15.
101. There are also parallels with other Gnostic gospels, such as saying 2, which echoes the Gospel of the Hebrews 6b. See *The Complete Gospels*, pp.305 & 433.
102. This saying recurs in modified form as an inscription in a mosque in Fatehpur Sikri, India: 'Jesus said, "This world is a bridge. Pass over it, but do not build your dwelling there."' The link between the Gospel of Thomas and Fatehpur Sikri could be Thomas himself, who is

traditionally held to be the apostle who went east and evangelised India.

103. II Corinthians 2–4. Good News Bible version. For an in-depth study of how the Gnostics read Paul, see Elaine Pagels, *The Gnostic Paul: Gnostic Exegesis of the Pauline Letters* (Trinity Press, 1992).

104. The Treatise on the Resurrection, *Nag Hammadi Library in English*, p.55.

105. The Treatise on the Resurrection, *Nag Hammadi Library in English*, p.56.

106. The Gospel of Philip, *The Gnostic Bible*, p.276.

107. The Gospel of Philip, *Nag Hammadi Library in English*, p.144.

108. The Gospel of Philip, *Nag Hammadi Library in English*, p.153.

109. The Gospel of Philip, *Nag Hammadi Library in English*, p.144. The use of Paul's words here is a classic example of how Gnostic writers used the arguments of others for their own purposes.

110. Elaine Pagels recounts such an interpretation in *Beyond Belief*, p.74.

111. The Gospel of Philip, *The Gnostic Bible*, p.273.

112. The Gospel of Philip, *The Gnostic Bible*, p.261.

113. The Gospel of Philip, *The Gnostic Bible*, p.260.

114. The Gospel of Philip, *The Gnostic Bible*, p.279.

115. The Gospel of Philip, *The Gnostic Bible*, p.272.

116. The Gospel of Philip, *The Gnostic Bible*, p.273.

117. The Gospel of Philip, *The Gnostic Bible*, p.283.

118. The Gospel of Philip, *The Gnostic Bible*, p.266.

119. The Gospel of Philip, *The Gnostic Bible*, p.273.

120. The Gospel of Philip, *The Gnostic Bible*, p.266.

121. The Gospel of Philip, *The Gnostic Bible*, p.267.

122. The Gospel of Philip, *The Gnostic Bible*, p.273.

123. The Gospel of Mary, *The Nag Hammadi Library in English*, p.525.

124. The Gospel of Mary, *The Gnostic Bible*, p.479.

125. The Gospel of Mary, *The Nag Hammadi Library in English*, p.525.

126. The Gospel of Mary, *The Gnostic Bible*, p.479.

127. The Gospel of Mary, *The Gnostic Bible*, p.479.

128. The Gospel of Mary, *The Gnostic Bible*, p.481.

129. The Gospel of Mary, *The Gnostic Bible*, p.481.

130. *The Complete Gospels*, p.357.

131. *The Complete Gospels*, p.358.

132. Thunder: Perfect Mind, *The Gnostic Bible*, p.226.

133. Thunder: Perfect Mind, *The Gnostic Bible*, pp.226–7.

134. Introduction to Thunder: Perfect Mind, *The Gnostic Bible*, p.225.

135. Elaine Pagels, *The Gnostic Gospels*.

136. The Exegesis on the Soul, *The Gnostic Bible*, p.407.

137. The Exegesis on the Soul, *The Gnostic Bible*, p.407. The quote from Paul is from Ephesians 6:12.

138. The Exegesis on the Soul, *The Gnostic Bible*, pp.409–10.

139. The Exegesis on the Soul, *The Gnostic Bible*, pp.410–11.

140. The Exegesis on the Soul, *The Gnostic Bible*, p.411.

141. The other books in the Askew Codex are Extracts from the Books of the Saviour and the Book of the Great Logos.

142. Pistis Sophia 2 (GRS Mead translation).

143. Pistis Sophia 17.

144. Pistis Sophia 72.

145. Pistis Sophia 72.

146. He does, however, lapse into his old ways and complains again that Mary is talking too much near the very end of Pistis Sophia, in Ch 148.

147. Pistis Sophia 102.

148. Pistis Sophia 125.

149. For a superb portrayal of the Church's fear of laughter, see Umberto Eco's *The Name of the Rose*, whose plot revolves around a treatise on comedy by Aristotle that comes to light in the library of a monastery in the Italian Alps. Jean Jacques Annaud's 1986 film adaptation starring Sean Connery is also well worth a watch.

150. He is also credited with writing, amongst others, the Acts of Thomas, which contains the well-known Gnostic allegory, the Hymn of the Pearl.

151. Not actually identified in the Acts of John as Gethsemane, but we can infer that this is the possible location from the context, which states that the scene takes place before Jesus is 'delivered up' to 'the lawless Jews'. See *The Apocryphal New Testament*, p.318.

152. The Acts of Thomas, *The Apocryphal New Testament*, p.318.

153. The Gospel of Philip, *The Gnostic Bible*, p.277.

154. The Gospel of Thomas, saying 108, *The Gnostic Bible*, p.68.

155. The Acts of Thomas, *The Apocryphal New Testament*, p.319.

156. The Acts of Thomas, *The Apocryphal New Testament*, p.321.

157. Sometimes known as the Gnostic or Coptic Apocalypse of Peter, not to be confused with the Apocalypse of Peter. For the non-Gnostic version, see *The Apocryphal New Testament*, pp.593–615.

158. The Apocalypse of Peter, *The Nag Hammadi Library in English*, p.377.

159. The Apocalypse of Peter, *The Nag Hammadi Library in English*, p.377.

160. Freke & Gandy, p.162.

161. Irenaeus, *Against Heresies* XXXI.

162. Epiphanius (Haeres., xxxviii).

163. For an in-depth study of the finding of the Gospel, see Krosney. A shorter account is given by Rodolphe Kasser in Rodolphe Kasser, Marvin Meyer & Gregor Wurst (Editors), *The Gospel of Judas* (National Geographic, 2006), pp.47–76.

164. The Gospel of Judas, *The Gospel of Judas*, pp. 22–3.

165. The Gospel of Judas, *The Gospel of Judas*, p.19.

166. The Gospel of Judas, *The Gospel of Judas*, p.22.

167. Plato, *Timaeus*, 41d–42b.

168. The Gospel of Judas, *The Gospel of Judas*, p.41.

169. The Gospel of Judas, *The Gospel of Judas*, p.43.

170. See The Gospel of Judas, *The Gospel of Judas*, p.44, footnote 147.

171. The Gospel of Judas, *The Gospel of Judas*, p.45.

172. Clement of Alexandria, *Stromata* VII, 104, 2.

173. This clause was actually added at the Second Ecumenical Council – Nicaea being the first – in 381.

174. Quoted in *The Nag Hammadi Library in English*, p.19.

175. This was not due to Athanasius's letter, however, but the orders of Roman Emperor Theodosius I.

176. The Gospel of the Egyptians, *The Nag Hammadi Library in English*, p.218.

177. The Church wasn't just persecuting Gnostic and dualist groups. At approximately the same time, other forms of non-dualist heresy – such as Pelagianism, which denied Original Sin – were quashed, in addition to other forms of Christianity that diverged from Rome, such as the Celtic and Nestorian churches. A case could be made for the former being the original form of Christianity in Europe, while the latter – despite persecution – persists to this day.

178. The word 'maniac' derives from a derogatory term for Manichaean.

179. See Yuri Stoyanov, *op. cit.*, p.103.

180. See Stoyanov, *ibid.*, pp.104–6.

181. Stoyanov, *ibid.*, p.170.

182. The chronicler Alan of Lille (*c.* 1128–1202) believed that 'Cathar' derived 'from the cat, because, it is said, they kiss the posterior of the cat, in whose form, as they say, Lucifer appears to them'. Such

charges were part of the Church's common arsenal of accusations against their enemies.

183. Wakefield & Evans, *Heresies of the High Middle Ages*, pp.126 32.

184. The Cathars did not reject the whole of the Old Testament, and continued to hold the Psalms, Job and the prophets in high regard.

185. This memorable description of the Perfect comes from Heinrich Fichtenau, quoted in Lambert. p.30.

186. There was also a small number of women troubadours, known as 'trobairitz'. In their songs, the object of desire was usually a man.

187. Roger Boase, *The Origin and Meaning of Courtly Love: A Critical Study of European Scholarship* (Manchester University Press, 1977), p.78.

188. Not all troubadours and trobairitz were anti-clerical: the trobairitz Gormonda de Montpellier 'associated with a Dominican community, [and] may have been lapsed Cathar' (Burl, Aubrey, *God's Heretics: The Albigensian Crusade*, p.10), whilst Foulques de Marseilles renounced the troubadour's life to become a Cistercian monk in 1195. Ten years later he was made Bishop of Toulouse.

189. Tobias Churton, *The Gnostic Philosophy*, p.182.

190. Churton *ibid.*, p.183.

191. Churton, *op.cit.*, p.184.

192. The Poimandres of Hermes Trismegistus, see Gilbert's 'Foreword' in Scott.

193. *Oration on the Dignity of Man*, quoted in Tobias Churton, *The Gnostics*, p.113.

194. The Acts of Peter, *The Apocryphal New Testament*, p.423.

195. Holroyd, *op. cit.*, p.93.

196. Edward Gibbon, *The Decline and Fall of the Roman Empire*, XV.

197. Richard Smith, 'The Modern Relevance of Gnosticism', *The Nag Hammadi Library in English*, p.532.

198. Smith, *The Nag Hammadi Library in English*, p.535.

199. Kathleen Raine in conversation with Tobias Churton, 1986, quoted in Churton, *op cit.*, p.143.

200. Quoted in Churton, *op. cit.*, p.149.

201. Hoeller, *op. cit.*, p.211.

202. Quoted in Hoeller, *op. cit.*, p.169. Jung felt that Rudolph Steiner's Anthroposophy was also similarly Gnostic. Steiner was originally a Theosophist, but left to form his own school in 1912 after a falling out with one of Madame Blavatsky's successors, the writer and social reformer Annie Besant.

203. The Rosicrucians, the Yezidis and Luciferian witches, amongst others, are also fundamentally Gnostic.

204. Stephan Hoeller, *The Gnostic Jung and the Seven Sermons to the Dead*, p.8.

205. Hoeller, *ibid.*, pp.8–9.

206. Hoeller, *op. cit.*, p.8.

207. The First Sermon, Hoeller, *op. cit.*, p.47.

208. The First Sermon, Hoeller, *op. cit.*, p.47.

209. The First Sermon, Hoeller, *op. cit.*, p.47.

210. e.g. In his Introduction to 'The Secret of the Golden Flower', *Collected Works*, Vol. 13, pp.1–56 (Princeton University Press, 1968).

211. Hoeller, *op. cit.*, p.38.

212. Hermann Hesse, *Steppenwolf*, quoted in Smith, 'The Modern Relevance of Gnosticism', *The Nag Hammadi Library in English*, p.541.

213. Gnostic themes have been utilised by Lawrence Durrell, in his *Alexandria Quartet*, Jack Kerouac in *Dr Sax*, Anatole France in *The Revolt of the Angels*, Harold Bloom in *The Flight to Lucifer*, Allen Ginsberg in *Plutonian Ode*, amongst others, and also in the work of Borges and Cioran.

214. *Moby-Dick*, Ch 119.

215. Walter H Sokel, 'Between Gnosticism and Jehovah: The Dilemma in Kafka's Religious Attitude', *The Allure of Gnosticism*, p.147.

216. Sokel, p.153, quoting from Kafka's notebooks.

217. Sokel, p.157, quoting from Kafka's notebooks.

218. See Erich Heller, 'The Castle: A Company of Gnostic Demons' in *Franz Kafka's The Castle: Critical Interpretations* (Chelsea House, 1988).

219. Bernard Sellin, The Life and Works of David Lindsay, p.227.

220. David Lindsay, *A Voyage to Arcturus*, pp.164–5. The concept that the lower, false world is still somehow real – 'not at all like a dream' – was reiterated by Aldous Huxley, who observed that while the world may ultimately be an illusion, it is nevertheless one that we must take seriously.

221. *Ibid.*, pp.195–6.

222. For instance, in Lindsay's second novel, *The Haunted Woman* (1922), the mysterious upper window at Runhill Court looks out onto a view of Anglo-Saxon England, which, in the context of the book, stands for the Sublime. In *Sphinx* (1923), the Sublime is visible in dreams, which Nicholas Cabot attempts to capture with his dream machine. *The Violet Apple* (written 1924–6, but not published until 1976) is Lindsay's thoroughly Gnostic take on the book of Genesis: when Anthony Kerr

and Haidee eat the apples that are said to be descendants of the fruit of the Tree in Eden, they can see people's true nature and the true nature of reality, which is 'a common coffin' (p.189). Lindsay likewise sees Adam's and Eve's eating of the fruit as the gaining of knowledge, 'an eternal symbol of the first resurrection from the dead – of the first rising of man and woman from a world of unconscious animals' (p.193). (The theme of resurrection is further stressed in that the novel is set over Easter.) This is in perfect accord with the Gnostics of classical antiquity – see Chapter 2. In Haidee, Lindsay introduces a powerful female character who is able to reveal spiritual truths, a theme taken up in his last two novels, *Devil's Tor* (1932) and *The Witch* (almost finished on his death in 1945, but not published until 1976).

223. David Power, *David Lindsay's Vision*, p.3.

224. David Lindsay, *Sketch Notes for a New System of Philosophy*, note 337.

225. The two novels referred to here are *Ubik* (1969) and *Radio Free Albemuth* (1985).

226. Philip K Dick, *VALIS*, Ch 6.

227. *VALIS*, Appendix, Note 29. The Empire, whilst also being the persecutors of the first Christians, can also be taken as the Roman Catholic Church, which persecuted the Gnostics.

228. This echoes Pascal's dictum that history is one man who learns continually. In PKD, the sense seems to be that we will all ultimately attain *gnosis*, a Valentinian idea.

229. *The Matrix* also draws on Buddhist ideas. See Frances Flannery-Dailey's & Rachel Wagner's essay *Wake Up! Gnosticism & Buddhism in The Matrix* at the Journal of Religion and Film's website, http://www.unomaha.edu/jrf/gnostic.htm.

230. The Gospel of Thomas, saying 25.

231. Murray Stein, 'The Gnostic Critique, Past and Present', in *The Allure of Gnosticism*, p.41.

232. Stein, *ibid.*, p.43.

233. The Treatise on the Resurrection, *Nag Hammadi Library in English*, p.56.

234. The Teachings of Silvanus, *The Nag Hammadi Library in English*, p.390.

235. Matthew 13.10–17, the William Tyndale translation. *Tyndale's New Testament* (Yale University Press, 1995), p 37. I am using Tyndale for these quotations because his version is arguably the most accurate in English, as his translation was the first English New Testament to be based on the original Greek.

236. *Ibid.*, p.37.
237. Mark 4.10–12 and Luke 8.9–10.
238. Mark 4.10–12, *Tyndale's New Testament*, *op. cit.*, p.66.
239. Matthew 6.1 and 6.6., *op. cit.*, p.27.
240. John Chapter 11, *op. cit.*, p.149.
241. The Secret Gospel of Mark, *The Complete Gospels*, *op. cit.*, p.411.

Suggestions for Further Reading

There are a great number of books dealing with Gnosticism and it is hoped that the following suggestions may help the curious reader navigate the considerable field of writings about Gnostics and Gnosticism.

Probably the most informed single volume about Gnosticism in English is Kurt Rudolph's *Gnosis: The Nature & History of Gnosticism*.

For a good starting point on the clash between Gnosticism and orthodoxy, see Elaine Pagels' now classic work, *The Gnostic Gospels*.

The standard edition of the Nag Hammadi library is that edited by James M Robinson, although good alternatives can be found in Bentley Layton's *The Gnostic Scriptures* and Barnstone and Meyer's *The Gnostic Bible*, which also includes Jewish, Islamic, Mandaean, Manichaean and Cathar texts in addition to those of antiquity.

Any reader wishing to deepen their understanding of Gnosticism as a spiritual practice should take a look at Stephan Hoeller's *Gnosticism: New Light on the Ancient Tradition of Inner Knowing* and June Singer's *Knowledge of the Heart: Gnostic Secrets of Inner Wisdom* (originally published as *A Gnostic Book of Hours*).

Finally, I would like to put a word in for the work of Philip K Dick. Perhaps his most obviously Gnostic book is *VALIS*, although Gnostic themes crop up throughout his oeuvre. Likewise, the work of David Lindsay, while a harder read than PKD, comes highly recommended.

Gnostic Scriptures

Barnstone, Willis & Meyer, Marvin (Editors), *The Gnostic Bible: Gnostic Texts of Mystical Wisdom from the Ancient and Medieval Worlds – Pagan, Jewish, Christian, Mandaean, Manichaean, Islamic and Cathar* (New Seeds, 2006)

Gardner, Iain & Lieu, Samuel NC (Editors), *Manichaean Texts from the Roman Empire* (Cambridge, 2004)

Kasser, Rodolphe, Meyer, Marvin & Wurst, Gregor (Editors), *The Gospel of Judas* (National Geographic, 2006)

King, Karen L, *The Gospel of Mary of Magdala* (Polebridge Press, 2003)

Klimkeit, Hans-Joachim, *Gnosis on the Silk Road: Gnostic Texts from Central Asia* (HarperCollins, 1993)

Layton, Bentley, *The Gnostic Scriptures* (Bantam, 1995)

Leloup, Jean-Yves, *The Gospel of Thomas: The Gnostic Wisdom of Jesus* (Bear & Co., 2005)

   The Gospel of Philip: Jesus, Mary Magdalene and the Gnosis of Sacred Union (Bear & Co., 2004)

   The Gospel of Mary Magdalene (Bear & Co., 2002)

Lidzbarski, Mark, *Mandaean Prayers and Hymns* (Living Water Books, 2002)

Mead, GRS (Editor/Translator), *Pistis Sophia: The Gnostic Tradition of Mary Magdalene, Jesus, and His Disciples* (Dover Publications, 2005)

Meyer, Marvin (Editor), *The Nag Hammadi Scriptures: The Revised and Updated Translation of Sacred Gnostic Texts Complete in One Volume* (HarperCollins, 2007)

Patterson, Stephen J, Robinson, James M and Bethge, Hans-Gebhard, *The Fifth Gospel: The Gospel of Thomas Comes of Age* (Trinity Press International, 1998)

Robinson, James M (General Editor), *The Nag Hammadi Library in English* (HarperCollins, 1990)

Scott, Walter (Editor/Translator), Gilbert, Adrian (Foreword), *Hermetica: The Writings Attributed to Hermes Trismegistus* (Solos Press, 1992)

Gnostic and Apocryphal Scriptures

Elliott, JK (Editor), *The Apocryphal New Testament* (Oxford, 1993)

Meyer, Marvin, *The Secret Gospels of Jesus: The Definitive Collection of Gnostic Gospels and Mystical Books about Jesus of Nazareth* (Darton, Longman and Todd, 2005; also published as *The Gnostic Gospels of Jesus*)

Miller, Robert J (Editor), *The Complete Gospels* (HarperCollins, 1994)

Gnosticism

Allison, Christine, *The Yezidi Oral Tradition in Iraqi Kurdistan* (Curzon Press, 2001)

SUGGESTIONS FOR FURTHER READING

Baker, Karen, *The Hidden Peoples of the World: The Mandaeans of Iraq: An exploration of the Mandaeans of Iraq: their history, beliefs, community organization and the effects of the 21st Century Diaspora* (VDM Verlag, 2009)

Blackman, EC, *Marcion and His Influence* (Wipf & Stock Publishers, 2004)

Blavatsky, HP, *On the Gnostics* (Point Loma Publications, 1994)

Buckley, Jorunn Jacobsen, *The Mandaeans: Ancient Texts and Modern People* (Oxford University Press, 2002)

Churton, Tobias, *The Gnostics* (Weidenfeld & Nicholson, 1987)
    The Gnostic Philosophy: From Ancient Persia to Modern Times (Signal Publishing, 2003)

Drower, ES, *The Mandaeans of Iraq and Iran: Their Cults, Customs, Magic Legends, and Folklore* (Gorgias Press, 2002)

Freke, Timothy & Gandy, Peter, *The Laughing Jesus: Religious Lies & Gnostic Wisdom* (Harmony Books, 2005)

Hoeller, Stephan A, *Gnosticism: New Light on the Ancient Tradition of Inner Knowing* (Quest Books, 2002)
    Jung and the Lost Gospels: Insights into the Dead Sea Scrolls and Nag Hammadi Library (Quest Books, 1989)
    The Gnostic Jung and the Seven Sermons to the Dead (Quest Books, 1985)

Holroyd, Stuart, *The Elements of Gnosticism* (Element Books, 1994)

Jonas, Hans, *The Gnostic Religion* (Beacon Press, 2001)

King, Karen L, *The Secret Revelation of John* (Harvard University Press, 2006)
    What is Gnosticism? (Harvard University Press, 2003)
    Images of the Feminine in Gnosticism (Alban Books, 2000)
    Revelation of the Unknowable God: A Gnostic Text from the Nag Hammadi Library (Polebridge Press, n.d.)

King, Karen L and Pagels, Elaine, *Reading Judas: The Gospel of Judas and the Shaping of Christianity* (Allen Lane, 2007)

Kreyenbroek, Philip G, *Yezidism – Its Background, Observances and Textual Tradition* (The Edwin Mellen Press, 1995)

Krosney, Herbert, *The Lost Gospel: The Quest for the Gospel of Judas Iscariot* (National Geographic, 2006)

Lupieri, Edmondo, *The Mandaeans: The Last Gnostics* (William B Eerdmans Publishing Company, 2002)

Mead, GRS, *Simon Magus: His Philosophy and Teachings* (Book Tree, 2003)
    Fragments of a Faith Forgotten (Kessinger Publishing, 1996)

Meyer, Marvin, *The Gnostic Discoveries: The Impact of the Nag Hammadi Library* (Longman and Todd, 2006)

Pagels, Elaine, *Beyond Belief: The Secret Gospel of Thomas* (Pan Books, 2005)

The Gnostic Paul: Gnostic Exegesis of the Pauline Letters (Trinity Press, 1992)

The Gnostic Gospels (Penguin Books, 1990)

The Johannine Gospel in Gnostic Exegesis: Heracleon's Commentary on John (Scholars Press, 1989)

Rudolph, Kurt, *Gnosis: The Nature & History of Gnosticism* (T&T Clark, 1983)

Scholem, Gershom, *Jewish Gnosticism, Merkabah Mysticism, and Talmudic Tradition* (Jewish Theological Seminary of America, 1960)

Segal, Robert A (Editor), *The Allure of Gnosticism: The Gnostic Experience in Jungian Psychology and Contemporary Culture* (Open Court, 1995)

Singer, June *Knowledge of the Heart: Gnostic Secrets of Inner Wisdom* (Element Books, 1999)

Van den Broek, Roelof and Hanegraaff, Wouter J (Editors), *Gnosis and Hermeticism from Antiquity to Modern Times* (State University of New York Press, 1998)

Related Interest

Ackroyd, Peter, *Blake* (Minerva, 1996)

Burl, Aubrey, *God's Heretics: The Albigensian Crusade* (Sutton Publishing, 2002)

Dan, Joseph, *Kabbalah: A Very Short Introduction* (Oxford University Press, 2006)

Dick, Philip K, *In Pursuit of VALIS: Selections from the Exegesis* (Underwood Miller, 1991)

The Divine Invasion (Vintage Books, 1991)

The Transmigration of Timothy Archer (Vintage Books, 1991)

VALIS (Vintage Books, 1991)

Durrell, Lawrence, *The Alexandria Quartet* (Faber & Faber, 2005)

Irwin, William (Editor), *More Matrix and Philosophy: Revolutions and Reloaded Decoded* (Open Court Publishing, 2005)

The Matrix and Philosophy: Welcome to the Desert of the Real (Open Court Publishing, 2002)

Jung, CG, *Memories, Dreams, Reflections* (Fontana Press, 1995)

Kafka, Franz, *The Castle* (Penguin Books, 2000)

Kerouac, Jack, *Doctor Sax* (HarperCollins, 2006)

Lindsay, David, *A Voyage to Arcturus* (Allison & Busby, 1986)

The Haunted Woman (Canongate, 1987)

Sphinx (Resonance Bookworks, 2009)

The Violet Apple (Sidgwick & Jackson, 1978)

Devil's Tor (Resonance Bookworks, 2009)

The Witch (Chicago Review Press, 1976)

Sketch Notes for a New System of Philosophy (unpublished MS held in the National Library of Scotland, Edinburgh)

Martin, Sean, *Alchemy & Alchemists* (Pocket Essentials, 2006)

The Cathars: The Most Successful Heresy of the Middle Ages (Pocket Essentials, 2005)

The Knights Templar: The History & Myths of the Legendary Military Order (Pocket Essentials, 2004)

Melville, Herman, *Moby Dick* (University of California Press, 1983)

Mirandola Pico della, *Oration on the Dignity of Man* (Regnery Publishing, 1996)

Pick, JB, Wilson, Colin and Visiak, EH, *The Strange Genius of David Lindsay* (John Baker, 1970)

Power, David, *David Lindsay's Vision* (Paupers' Press, 1991)

Raine, Kathleen, *Blake and Antiquity* (Routledge, 2002)

Sellin, Bernard, *The Life and Works of David Lindsay* (Cambridge University Press, 2007)

Shah, Idries, *The Way of the Sufi* (Penguin Books, 1974)

Starbird, Margaret, *The Woman with the Alabaster Jar: Mary Magdalen and the Holy Grail* (Bear & Co., 1993)

Stoyanov, Yuri, *The Hidden Tradition in Europe: The Secret History of Medieval Christian Heresy* (Penguin Books, 1994)

Vaughan-Lee, Llewellyn (Editor), *Travelling the Path of Love: Sayings of Sufi Masters* (The Golden Sufi Center, 1995)

Yeffeth, Glenn (Editor), *Taking the Red Pill: Science, Philosophy and Religion in 'The Matrix'* (Summersdale, 2003)

Weblinks

http://www.earlychristianwritings.com   Contains a wealth of texts, both orthodox and Gnostic, from the early centuries CE

http://egina2.blogspot.com/   The blog of Gnostic minister Jordan Stratford

http://gnoscast.blogspot.com/   The blog of Gnostic minister Troy Pierce

http://www.gnosis.org   The website of Ecclesia Gnostica, it also contains many Gnostic texts, articles and talks. The best place to start on the web for all things Gnostic

http://www.johannite.org/   The Johannite Church

http://www.mandaeanunion.org/index.htm/   The website of the Mandaean Union

http://www.palmtreegarden.org/   Describes itself as 'an online Gnostic community', PTG takes its name from the work of Philip K Dick

http://www.papyrology.ox.ac.uk/POxy/index.html   The Oxyrhynchus Papyri Project

http://www.phildickiangnosticism.com/   A site dedicated to Gnosticism in PKD's work

http://www.thegodabovegod.com/home.html   Home of Miguel Conner's excellent Aeon Byte gnostic radio show

http://www.yeziditruth.org/home   A good Yezidi resource, featuring news, history and sacred texts

Index

A SHORT HISTORY OF EUROPE

Gordon Kerr

What is Europe? Firstly, of course, it is a continent made up of countless disparate peoples, races and nations, and governed by different ideas, philosophies, religions and attitudes. Nonetheless, it has a common thread of history running through it, stitching the lands and peoples of its past and present together into one fabric. This narrative is welded together by the continent's great institutions, such as the Church of Rome, the Holy Roman Empire, the European Union, individual monarchies, trade organisations and social movements. At times they have prevented anarchy from destroying the achievements of the many great men and women the continent has produced. At other times, of course, it is these very institutions that have been at the heart of the war and strife that have threatened to reduce Europe to ruin on numerous occasions.

Europe, however, is also an idea. From almost the beginning of time, men have harboured aspirations to make this vast territory one. The Romans came close and a few centuries later, the foundations for a great European state were laid with the creation of the Holy Roman Empire – an empire different to any other in that it enjoyed the approval of God, through the Church in Rome. Napoleon overreached himself in attempting to create a European-wide Empire – as did Adolf Hitler. Now, however, Europe is as close as it ever has been to being one entity. The European Union is an ever-expanding club of which everyone in Europe wants to be a member, although, as the recent rejection of the European Constitution by the French and the Dutch, demonstrates, we Europeans still cling to our national independence.

THE CATHARS

Sean Martin

Catharism was the most successful heresy of the Middle Ages. Flourishing principally in the Languedoc and Italy, the Cathars taught that the world is evil and must be transcended through a simple life of prayer, work, fasting and non-violence. They believed themselves to be the heirs of the true heritage of Christianity going back to apostolic times, and completely rejected the Catholic Church and all its trappings, regarding it as the Church of Satan; Cathar services and ceremonies, by contrast, were held in fields, barns and in people's homes.

Finding support from the nobility in the fractious political situation in southern France, the Cathars also found widespread popularity among peasants and artisans. And again unlike the Church, the Cathars respected women, and women played a major role in the movement. Alarmed at the success of Catharism, the Church founded the Inquisition and launched the Albigensian Crusade to exterminate the heresy. While previous Crusades had been directed against Muslims in the Middle East, the Albigensian Crusade was the first Crusade to be directed against fellow Christians, and was also the first European genocide. With the fall of the Cathar fortress of Montségur in 1244, Catharism was largely obliterated, although the faith survived into the early fourteenth century.

Today, the mystique surrounding the Cathars is as strong as ever, and Sean Martin recounts their story and the myths associated with them in this lively and gripping book.

'An exemplary introduction... a clear account of Cathar beliefs and rituals.' Sir Christopher Bland, *The Sunday Telegraph*

To order your copy
£9.99 including free postage and packing
(UK and Republic of Ireland only)
£10.99 for overseas orders

For credit card orders phone 0207 430 1021 (ref KT)

For orders by post – cheques payable to Oldcastle Books,
21 Great Ormond Street, London, WC1N 3JB
www.noexit.co.uk

THE KNIGHTS TEMPLAR

Sean Martin

The Knights Templar were the most powerful military religious order of the Middle Ages. Formed to protect pilgrims in the Holy Land, they participated in the Crusades and rapidly gained wealth, lands and influence and were answerable to none save the Pope himself.

In addition to having a fearful military reputation, they were also Christendom's first bankers – inventing much of the modern banking system that is still in use today – and were also involved in exploration and engineering.

Seemingly untouchable for nearly two centuries, the Templars fell from grace spectacularly after the loss of the Holy Land: in 1307, all Templars in France were arrested on charges of heresy, homosexuality, denial of the cross and devil worship. The order was suppressed by the Pope in 1312, and Jacques de Molay, the last Grand Master, was burnt at the stake as a heretic two years later.

The myth of the Templars was born and in the ensuing seven centuries, they have exerted a unique influence over European history: orthodox historians see them as nothing more than soldier-monks whose arrogance was their ultimate undoing, while others see them as occultists of the first order, the founders of Freemasonry, possessors of the Holy Grail and the Turin Shroud.

'A well written and easily enjoyed introduction to the history of this extra-ordinary crusading Order of military monks whose account still manages to fascinate even after all this time.' Michael Baigent, *Freemasonry Today*

'Do not be deceived by the book's seeming brevity. For this book contains more information than many recent books on the Templars weighing in at three to four times this one.' Stephen Dafoe, *Templar History*

To order your copy
£7.99 including free postage and packing
(UK and Republic of Ireland only)
£9.99 for overseas orders

For credit card orders phone 0207 430 1021 (ref KT)

For orders by post – cheques payable to Oldcastle Books,
21 Great Ormond Street, London, WC1N 3JB
www.noexit.co.uk